a *Pearl* formed by adversity

a Pearl formed by adversity

Margaret Ann Miller

For His Glory

Margaret A. Miller

Printed in the United States of America

Publishing services by Selah Publishing Group, LLC, Tennessee. The views expressed or implied in this work do not necessarily reflect those of Selah Publishing Group.

ISBN: 978-1-58930-274-7
Library of Congress Control Number: 2011911484

For Marv
My loving husband and a profound example of true and unwavering dedication.

1989, Jolene, Marv, me, Julie

Acknowledgments

My heartfelt thanks goes to all those whom God sent my way to keep me writing my story. I received amazing encouragement from so many people. The ladies who join me in Bible study classes, friends and acquaintances, relatives from near and far, and even people I don't personally know have spurred me on. Whenever fear or doubt or apathy invaded, one of God's special messengers appeared with kind and supportive words that sustained me during this God-ordained task.

But my greatest encourager was my cousin Margie. I had prayed that God would send someone to come alongside me, someone who would truly grasp my story, understand my intention in sharing it, and relate to my heart. He gave me Margie. Even though miles separate us physically, God graciously placed our hearts side-by-side. I had a story to tell, and she had the God-given gift of writing. She became my hands and arms and legs with her computer skills, her mastery of words, and her ability to develop thoughts clearly. It is because of her help that my story is before you.

I so enjoyed my journey with Margie on this project. Together, we laughed and cried; we wrote and rewrote; we inspired and challenged each other; we waited, and we prayed; and we took huge steps of faith. To be known and to be loved is a tremendous gift. Thank you, Margie, from the depths of my heart.

And thank You, God, for loving me, guiding me, enabling me, and for being my ultimate Great Encourager.

—Margaret

Preface

My hope and prayer is that each one who reads my brief story will be able to embrace God and be strengthened in his or her personal relationship with our Savior, Jesus Christ. Throughout the Old Testament, people built altars and piled up rocks as reminders of all the Lord had done for them. This is my pile of rocks, my altar, laid before you and the Lord, in thankfulness for all He has done.

—Margaret

Encouragement

The journey Margaret has traveled throughout her lifetime is not particularly special. The tough times and challenges that she's experienced are not entirely different from yours and mine. She's not the only person who's been physically paralyzed as a result of an automobile accident. And she's not the only person whose life has been turned around by the grace of God.

In fact, if you change the names and modify the scenarios, this could be your story. *A Pearl* is an illustration of God's magnificence in comparison to man's depravity. It's a story of one who was blind, but now can see. And it's a vivid portrayal of despair transformed into hope.

I've often quipped that "ignorance is bliss" (especially when my children were teenagers), but ignorance is never bliss when it comes to knowing Jesus. If Christ is Lord of your life, then *A Pearl* will challenge you to deepen your relationship and dependence on Him and trigger some thoughtful reflection on your growth in Christ. And if Christ is not Lord of your life, then be prepared to meet Him in the following pages.

A Pearl is the true story of how Margaret was radically changed, both physically and spiritually, as a result of a devastating automobile accident. It wasn't written to invoke pity or sorrow for her or to encourage only those who identify with her physical limitations. It was written solely to show the magnitude of God's love for His people and to expose His unfathomable power available to all who believe in Him. It was written to demonstrate that there are no boundaries to all He can do in a person's life—no matter the sin, the regret, the sorrow, the anger, the fear, or the despair a heart may harbor.

Some Scripture verses are included, not only to reveal how they specifically applied to Margaret's transformation, but also to encourage you to pause and consider how they may apply to your life or circumstances. Allow them to lay bare the magnitude of God's love and power, and His amazing grace and mercy.

As you read through Margaret's journey, consider your own life's journey. Reflect on your beginning and travel through the ups and downs that life has presented along the way. Then evaluate how you've grown, whom you've depended on, and what or whom your hope is based upon for tomorrow. Perhaps you'll be able to relate to the profound difference God made in Margaret's life and how He used her struggles and frailty to unveil His power and unconditional love.

Nothing in *A Pearl* is fabricated. None of the names have been changed, and none of the scenarios have been exaggerated. It is a true story from start to finish that depicts how God worked in Margaret's life. That kind of story doesn't need embellishment. It's powerful on its own.

As well, the truth of Margaret is that she isn't any different from you and me. But she is the epitome of what God can do in someone's life, and she exudes the fruit of the Spirit.

> *But the fruit of the Spirit is love, joy, peace, patience, kindness, goodness, faithfulness, gentleness, self-control; against such things there is no law.*
> —Galatians 5:22-23

God used the changes He made in Margaret's life to draw me to Him. In her I saw a gentleness and peace that I didn't understand, but I knew I wanted. I'll never forget the day she sat in her wheelchair at my dad's bedside just days before he died and quietly asked if he knew Jesus. She said it was important to find out. I thought her concern was sweet because everything about Margaret was always sweet and genuine. But I didn't truly understand the magnitude of her question until about nine months later—nine months later when Jesus came into my heart and changed me forever.

I thank God for all the "Margarets" in the world—they are truly pearls of great price.

> *Yes, if you call out for insight and raise your voice for understanding, if you seek it like silver and search for it as for hidden treasures, then you will understand the fear of the LORD and find the knowledge of God. For the LORD gives wisdom; from his mouth come knowledge and understanding.*
> —Proverbs 2:3–6

—Margie Hinson

CONTENTS

Do you remember a time when you couldn't make sense of your life or your circumstances? Can you recall ever feeling so frightened or confused that you couldn't move and couldn't think? Can you imagine such a feeling?

How were you raised? What were your family's values? Have they changed or been redirected as a result of your relationship with God? What are some of your earliest beliefs about your value as a person and whom do you credit for them?

Does the way in which you live your life outside your home match the way you live your life within the walls of your home?

What are some of the choices you made as a young adult, and how have they impacted your life? In retrospect, are there things you'd do differently today?

Do you insist on maintaining control of all aspects of your life? Are there areas that you won't relinquish to God? What is holding you back?

If you're a parent, think of your children. If not, think of
your parents. As a family, do you pull together to make your
home happy regardless of finances and obstacles? Is being
together what matters most?

Is your spouse the one who completes you or competes
with you? In retrospect, was the focus of your wedding an
intimate celebration of two lives becoming one or something
more superficial? Have you experienced the reality that
marriage is much more than just living together?

Have you ever thought that life was just not worth the pain,
the heartache, and the disappointment that it brings? Have
you ever been in a situation when you thought life couldn't
be more heart-wrenching—and then it was? How did you
respond? Where did you find your answer?

When did you first experience the difference that Jesus
makes in your life? Whom did God use to draw you to Him?
Do you remember the joy and the freedom you experienced
those first days and months as a born-again Christian? Do
you still rest in Jesus' strength and wisdom and simultaneously yearn for more?

What's the most humbling thing that's happened to you at
church? Were you able to laugh at it?

When have you experienced something embarrassing that
brought unwanted attention to you? Can you laugh at
your shortcomings with friends, or do you get angry and
defensive?

Do you tire of caring for others? Does your attitude reflect
joy in being able and available to help, or do you resent
the inconvenience? Does your answer reflect that you are
dependent on yourself or God?

A Lost Relationship

*Do you remember a time when you couldn't make sense
of your life or your circumstances? Can you recall ever
feeling so frightened or confused that you couldn't move
and couldn't think? Can you imagine such a feeling?*

I was twenty-eight years old. In fact, I'd just celebrated my birthday a few weeks earlier, on November 14th. I was a single mom who'd made a few poor choices that resulted in a few more downs than ups in my life, but things were finally falling into place.

By my standards, I was successful. I was a hard worker, attractive, and intent on doing my best to meet the needs of my family, friends, and business associates. I went to church some Sundays and knew a little bit about God. I figured that if I kept on my current path I'd probably make it to heaven when I died. I was, after all, a good person.

I was finally in control of my life, and it felt good. And on this December night, I felt especially good because a dinner date with an old flame had rekindled our relationship.

I was lighthearted and happy as I left the restaurant and headed down the two-lane country road to pick up my daughters from their grandmother's house. Julie was eight years old and Jolene was six, and they were no doubt playing on the floor in front of the special closet that stored all the fun toys their grandmother kept for them.

Jolene recalls the details of that night.

"*There is a closet in the entryway of my grandmother's house that is full of toys for all the grandkids to play with. There are many memories tucked away in that closet that I will never forget.*

"*I was sitting on the floor of the living room with all the toys spread out around me when the phone rang. Of course, I paid no attention to it because I was a typical child whose mind concentrated on only one activity at a time. The aroma of a home-baked meal flowed through the house as Grandma hummed along doing the busywork that grandmas do. The clock on the mantel ticked softly, repetitiously. It was Christmastime and spirits were high. Grandma unhurriedly answered the phone with a friendly and eager, 'Hello!'*

"*Then the feeling in the room changed ever-so-slowly from warm, comfortable, and cheery to disbelief, terror, and tears. As she hung up the phone, the tone of her voice as she began to speak told a story in itself ... somewhere, somehow, something was not right....*"

Jolene was right. Something was terribly wrong.

I wasn't far from my mother-in-law's home when a drunk driver out of control of his car rammed my car bumper and forced me into a ditch. Immediately I was the one out of control. Just a few miles and a few minutes ago, I had been on top of the world, but now the world was crashing down on me ... and on my girls.

"*Gently and caringly, Grandma informed my sister and me that our mother had been in an accident on her way to pick us up, and she was put in a hospital ... I knew nothing better than to burst into tears. No matter what Grandma said to reassure me, I could not contain myself. This was too unreal for me to comprehend.*

"*Now, that once-friendly, comforting clock on the mantel tick-tocked its way through anxiety and pain. We sat there on the couch, adorned with swollen cheeks and red, watery eyes, staring into space, each of our minds unable to escape thoughts of the accident and what condition our mommy was in.*

"*What should we do? How should we respond? Why was this happening? We wondered how all this could be true. Mommies were supposed to be indestructible and always available and able to take care of their children.*

"*My childlike mind was so afraid.*"

And while my daughters were trying to make sense of their situation, I was doing the same. In the blink of an eye, the carefree giddiness in my heart was replaced with stillness, stillness unlike any I'd ever known. In a split second the control I had over every aspect of my life was replaced with complete helplessness, helplessness beyond what I'd ever imagined.

On that night, I learned just how unpredictable life can be. As I drove, I had looked forward to picking up my girls, and I had anticipated the renewal of my relationship with Marv. All the while, another precious relationship was about to be lost forever: the relationship between my mind and my body.

December 20, 1975, is the date my spinal cord was crushed, and life as I'd known it would never be the same. It signifies tragedy and a tearing apart of my body. It marks the finish line of the only race in life I'd known how to run—a race run and won by hard work and self-sufficiency.

I didn't realize it at the time, but I was at the starting point of a completely new race—one that is run and won through total dependency on God. This date marks the beginning of the crumbling of the beliefs and ideals that formed the shaky foundation on which I'd built my life. It was the starting line of a new life and a very long, very challenging, but ultimately very wonderful journey in search of a beautiful pearl of great price.

As I wrote this book and reflected on my life, both before and after that pivotal date, I realized that although I often felt like I was the only one who experienced such shattering events, the reality is that everyone experiences tragedy in one way or another. I'm certain that only a small number of you reading this have been physically paralyzed, but I'm also certain that a great number of you have suffered or continue to suffer some degree of mental, emotional, or spiritual paralysis. We all do. And many times these bruises and injuries begin in childhood.

This is just my story, but if you read between the lines, you may find bits and pieces of yourself, your struggles, and your victories in these pages, as well.

1956, Our family of Five
Maureen, Mom, Mark, Dad, me

Through the Eyes of a Child

How were you raised? What were your family's values?
Have they changed or been redirected as a result of your
relationship with God? What are some of your earliest
beliefs about your value as a person and whom
do you credit for them?

When I was a little girl, all the outward appearances of my family resembled a typical 1950s *Father Knows Best* household. Dad was a successful second-generation jeweler who worked diligently, tirelessly, and constantly. He was rarely at home. Mom was a stay-at-home mom until I was eight years old, and then she joined forces with Dad and worked at the store. When I was born, the population of my hometown of Santa Maria, California, was less than 15,000 people. It was the perfect size for many people to know a little too much about other people's business without too much difficulty.

I'm the middle child of three. Mark is the baby, a couple of years younger than me, and Maureen is just eleven months older. It must have been terribly difficult for Mom to give birth to two daughters when she was just twenty-five years old. I've been told that she cried throughout her pregnancy with me. In fact, my parents reminded me on every birthday that I wasn't planned. I was a mistake. I'm sure they were teasing, but as a little girl, the words hurt.

For most of my life, I believed I was nothing more than a slipup. Every time I did something wrong, or disobeyed, or misbehaved, the recording in my mind automatically played, *You shouldn't have been born. You are a mistake.*

It wasn't until I became an adult that I realized the potential impact that a few words can have on a person—especially a child. I don't know if my parents' comments—that I was a mistake and responsible for my mother's nine months of misery—caused my quiet and shy personality, but I do know they had a long-lasting and profound effect on my sense of self-worth. I didn't become outwardly resentful and bitter; I just quietly internalized the words until they became the driving force in my life. *You shouldn't have been born. You are a mistake,* seemed to whisper through the wind, and the wind seemed to grow stronger and steadier through the years.

Fortunately, I had a protected and calm refuge across the street in the home of Dad's parents, Nana and Grandpa. I treasured my visits there because it meant that I could play on the swings in their backyard and spend time engrossed in Nana's garden. I can still see her beautiful array of roses, dahlias, and begonias. I remember how I loved to gobble up her delicious hot-milk coffee cakes as soon as they popped out of the oven. And I still remember sitting on the yellow bar stool in her kitchen and listening to her canary singing on the porch.

Nana's home was cozy and cheerful because Nana was cozy and cheerful. She exuded unconditional love and acceptance. I knew before I got in the door that she'd drown me with hugs and affection as only she could do. I knew I could count on her for yummy goodies and special treatment, but most of all, I knew I could count on her to listen. She listened to whatever I rambled on about. She never lost her temper, she never rushed me out the door no matter how long I babbled on, and she always accepted me just as I was. I crossed the street to my special cove as often as I could.

Nana was my never-changing, ever-reliable pillar before I knew Jesus. Her home was my shelter from the wind. I thrived on her bits of tenderness and morsels of attentive nonjudgmental listening.

Sadly, when I was about six, we moved across town into the house that eventually became known as simply "419," and Nana's safe haven was no longer across the street. Instead, the Miller Street School was across the street. And instead of a chirping canary and Nana's warm hugs enticing me to come over, there was a clanging school bell and dreaded classes summoning me to cross the street each morning.

School was always a struggle for me. The only subjects I excelled in were daydreaming and socializing. Maureen was the star student in our family. She excelled in academics, piano lessons, drama classes, and almost everything she attempted. She was always the best, and I couldn't begin to compete with her.

And then one day, Dad told me I was pretty. That one quick comment seemed to make life fall into place for me. With those few words, I was transformed from a ne'er-do-well to a winner. My appearance could be my ticket to success. I didn't have to take a test or compete with anyone else. In fact, my triumph was confirmed when I was voted the prettiest girl in high school.

I'd found my niche. Maureen could be the best. I could be pretty. And of course—Mark was the boy!

I didn't become conceited and pretentious a result of Dad's compliment, and I don't know if it had any impact on some of the choices and decisions I made. But I do know that as I focused on my outward appearance, I drifted along on the winds that led to a false and superficial sense of security.

After we moved away from Nana's protective cove, my visits with her became more sporadic. I couldn't see her home, I couldn't hear her voice, and I couldn't feel her reassuring warmth. She'd become somewhat inaccessible, and I missed her terribly. But life went on, and I managed as best I could on my own strength and in my own wisdom.

Still, when she wasn't close by, something was curiously missing in my heart. I relied heavily on the memories of those precious times with her. She had been my source of tender loving care that my heart needed to keep it pliable. Her soft hands of love had been my strength, and her open arms of compassion had been my refuge in those formative years of my life.

Nevertheless, just a couple of comments during my childhood formed the cornerstone of a belief system that I adhered to for many years. They weren't spoken in anger, and they weren't derogatory. In fact, they were said in jest. But somehow, deep within me, one caused me to feel like a mistake, and one convinced me that outward beauty can bring success. I carried those beliefs with me for years.

Prom Night 1964

Within the Walls

*Does the way in which you live your life outside
your home match the way you live your life
within the walls of your home?*

Within the walls of our home we all worked hard to live an idyllic family life. Manners were very important. Emily Post's book on etiquette was always our reference for entertaining and proper behavior in specific situations. We hosted many parties and entertained regularly. Mom enrolled Maureen and me in dramatic art classes so we'd know how to walk with perfect posture, how to properly pronounce words, and how to recite long dramatic stories. I took advantage of my training by doing some modeling in high school.

Anything and everything on display was very important in my family. The appearance of Dad's store, our home, and how Maureen, Mark, and I behaved at all times had to be just so. We were instilled with the admirable values of hard work, respect, and responsibility. Within the walls of our beautiful home we were a conservative, upper-middle-class, all-American family taking one day at a time. All my needs and many of my wants were supplied.

But when Mom started working at Dad's store, life changed dramatically. Everything still appeared as if our family fit the ideal mold of a 1950s sitcom, but in actuality, alcohol had intruded on us and was wreaking havoc on our lives.

I was in the third grade when Mom and Dad started drinking cocktails routinely with several friends after work. Since they all lived close by, cocktails and highballs often evolved into dinners together. Their social drinking continued throughout the years I attended high school. Dad always drank one scotch and an occasional glass of wine with dinner. He was always in control. But when it came to drinking, Mom was always out of control.

Whether or not we had guests, all our evening meals were served in the formal dining room and proper dress was required. No sweats or curlers were allowed. Our meal was always delicious, but Mom always drank too much and that ruined everything for everyone. It broke my heart because she was so loving and fun during the day and so difficult to love during the evening. She was still my mom, and I still loved her, but when she drank she changed. When she drank, she became some other woman whom I didn't know. It was as if this strange person pushed my real mom behind a tall barricade and hid her. My real, loving mom was unapproachable and unreachable when alcohol took hold of her.

And because I still clung to the belief that I was a mistake and everything that went wrong was my fault, I naturally assumed that I was the problem, and I had to fix it. So I cleaned house, washed clothes, fixed dinner, and did anything I could to try to ease Mom's load. Still, she drank.

Out of desperation I asked Dad if we could find help for her, and he immediately denied her problem and told me never to bring it up again. "There is no problem," he said. "We're strong and persevering." If we ever did have a problem, the solution was always: Take a Bufferin. Go to your room. And come out happy. Problems were buried, not confronted. Father knew best.

I don't know why Mom drank so much. Maybe she felt pressured to be the perfect wife and mother according to society's standards, and maybe those pressures mounted during the day and alcohol seemed to set her free in the evening. Maybe she was trying to earn acceptance and admiration from her peers. I truly don't know. But I do know that no matter the reason behind her uncontrolled drinking, it was far from being her source of freedom.

In fact, rather than freeing her, alcohol held her captive. The more she consumed, the more it consumed her and the more inaccessible she became. To me, alcohol was an insurmountable barrier to her love. No matter how many dirty clothes and dirty dishes I washed, I couldn't break down the wall. No matter how many shelves I dusted and dirty floors I swept, I couldn't reach her heart.

I was trying to earn her love, and my efforts were futile. It was a terrible feeling. There was an empty place in my heart that only she could fill. My heart ached, but I plodded along. I did my best and worked hard to please and obey my folks.

Part of obeying Mom and Dad included attending Mormon seminary with Maureen every morning before school. I never became an authority on Mormonism, but I learned that salvation was achieved by doing good works—lots and lots of good works.

For a year or so we dutifully went to church every Sunday morning as a family, but eventually Mom and Dad stayed in bed and read the paper while the three of us kids went to worship services.

I didn't like church. It was cold, scary, and lifeless. And to top things off, nothing in any of my lessons in Mormonism offered me any hope or solutions to help me help Mom. I had no idea that all my good intentions and hard work weren't going to cure Mom's disease or the ache in my heart. The only thing I knew was that I had to keep my nose to the grindstone and work, and then work some more. And I had to do it without complaining. I had to figure things out on my own and trust that my conclusions were correct.

By the time I was eighteen years old, I was used to relying on myself and convinced that all the conclusions I'd drawn were exactly right. The problem was that some of my conclusions were wrong. I'd believed a few words here and there and built my foundation for living on them. But I was building my foundation on lies, and like building a castle on the sand, it was doomed to collapse.

I believed that I was a mistake. I believed that I had to be pretty to succeed. I believed that I caused Mom's drinking, so I had to fix it. And I believed that I had to earn my way to salvation.

All these deceptions worked together to make me an extremely codependent, people-pleasing person. This flimsy foundation of lies played out in my life and caused fear, doubt, and despair. And as these unhealthy mind-sets churned beneath the sandy surface of my foundation, cracks began to form—cracks that would eventually result in total destruction.

As a teenager

Growing Years

*What are some of the choices you made as a young adult,
and how have they impacted your life? In retrospect,
are there things you'd do differently today?*

*J*ust a few months after my high school graduation, a blind date in
the form of a mountainous six-foot-five hunk of fun and frolic
popped into my life. His name was Bill. He swept me off my feet, and
I fell in love.

Bill and I were crazy about each other. We dated for the duration
of our year at junior college, and when we later transferred to different universities in southern California, we kept our relationship
alive through weekend phone calls. It wasn't a perfect setup, but our
relationship remained okay. The problem was that I wasn't okay.

I'd only been in school two months when constant nausea caused
me to seek medical help. I thought I was just terribly homesick—but
I was pregnant. The doctor who saw me was especially kind and did
his best to reassure me and comfort me. He even invited me to his
home for dinner. But even so, tears welled up in my eyes.

The thought of going home to tell my folks this shameful news
terrified me. I went to a cliff overlooking the ocean and stood there in
a daze, desperately staring. I thought about jumping, but I couldn't.
It's kind of funny, but one of the reasons I couldn't make myself jump

was that I'd accepted the doctor's invitation to dinner. His great love and compassion compelled me to keep my promise.

The bottom line was that I knew I had to choose life and face the disgrace I would cause to our upstanding family name. Suddenly our small town felt even smaller. I had nowhere to run and nowhere to hide.

Bill came to get me, and we made the seemingly endless drive home together.

Mom's remark to our announcement was, "So, now you're just going to be a mom." Then as I lay in bed that night, I heard Dad in the next room sobbing hysterically.

In the midst of my parents' grief, cousin Lucy called and soothed their burdened hearts with a single comment. "Just love her," she said. And love was what I needed so desperately. I was mortified at how I'd let them down, and I vowed to never again disappoint them. My life would focus on pleasing my parents.

Bill and I quit school and got married right away. It was October 1966. We not only wanted to get married, it was the only proper thing to do. In those days, having a baby out of wedlock was even more disgraceful than conceiving one out of wedlock. Mom and Dad insisted on a prompt wedding, and I'm sure Emily Post would have agreed.

Julie was born in May 1967. She was beautiful, fragile, and petite. Bill and I adored her and loved our new role as parents. We moved to a beautiful five-acre plot a few miles outside Santa Maria in 1968, and in 1969 our precious daughter Jolene was born.

We loved our little slice of land, and we lived off everything we produced. We had pigs, goats, chickens, fruit trees, and a sizable organically grown vegetable garden. And right smack-dab in the middle of our delicious tomato patch we grew marijuana. We were, in fact, very proud of our organically grown stash!

During this season of my life, I attended a Presbyterian church with Nana. Although Bill was with me when the girls were dedicated to the Lord, he didn't typically accompany me to church no matter how much I pleaded. It felt good to be in church, but not good enough to live a life pleasing to God during the week.

We smoked pot and cigarettes and drank alcohol in an attempt to hide our hurts, our pains, and our loneliness. It's no surprise that those crutches didn't solve any of our problems. And to top things off, my pledge to please Mom and Dad was a disservice to Bill and contributed even more to the erosion of our marriage.

We divorced in 1973, leaving a trail of adultery and betrayal behind.

In Control

Do you insist on maintaining control of all aspects of your life? Are there areas that you won't relinquish to God? What is holding you back?

After our divorce, I became a very independent woman. I raised my girls (who were now eight and six years old) and worked full-time managing Dad's gift shop that was adjacent to his jewelry store. Transitioning each day from work mode to mom mode was challenging for me, so I sought peace in the rituals of Eastern religions. I practiced meditation and chanted my mantra to a maharishi guru.

I was in control of all aspects of my life, and I was happy.

In addition to managing the gift shop, I offered a window-dressing service to other merchants, one of which was a scuba shop located just a few doors down the street. That was where I met Marv. We were very attracted to each other and dated awhile. But as our relationship developed, we tried to mold each other into someone we weren't, so we parted ways. Then, about six months later, Marv decided he wanted to give our relationship another chance. It was during the busy Christmas holidays when we met for dinner, reconnected, and made a date for New Year's Eve.

I was happy when I left the restaurant that night. I'd achieved a new level of independence, self-confidence, and success. I'd managed to recover from a failed marriage and orchestrated a sense of normalcy in my life. My plans and purposes were finally in place. Life was good.

It was about 8 P.M. when Marv and I finished our meal that night. He headed home, and I headed to pick up my girls from their grandmother's place, but I never made it.

That was December 20, 1975.

December 20, 1975

*Have you lost someone, has there been an event,
or a single day in time that dramatically
changed the rest of your life?*

One minute I was happily driving down the road, and the next minute I was being shoved down the road by another car—another car that was driving extremely fast. And the next thing I knew, I was upside-down in a ditch.

It happened so quickly. Nothing made sense. I felt myself spinning out of control in a whirlwind of confusion, as if I was leaving the earth. I saw my girls, my workplace, and my home. Leaving seemed okay because I wasn't leaving by my own strength. But at the same time, I somehow knew I was jammed upside-down in my crushed car. What I didn't know was that communication between my body and my mind was also jammed by my crushed spinal cord.

Then I remember hearing a familiar voice calling my name. It was Rosalie, a former employee of Dad's store. She and her husband had witnessed the accident and stopped to help, and I faintly heard her assuring me that more help was coming.

Most of the activity at the scene of the accident was surreal and foggy, but I'll never forget the strong smell of gasoline. After the rescue team arrived, I heard some of the men talking nervously about the possibility of a fire starting. Panic enveloped me as they struggled to remove me from my mangled car. They pushed and pulled for what seemed like an eternity. Finally, they broke the back window and pulled me through the opening to safety.

Once freed from my crushed car, I was strapped to a stretcher and repeatedly instructed not to move my neck. The ambulance attendant cautioned me to keep absolutely still throughout the entire drive to Marion Hospital.

I didn't know why they were they so adamant.

An eerie stillness swept over me. I felt only the beating of my heart and the rise and fall of my lungs. A deep inner shiver made my teeth chatter, and my body shook uncontrollably. I was in shock.

Once we arrived at the hospital, I remember lying flat on my back and looking at the ceiling. A single fire sprinkler hung above me. There were white ceilings, white walls, and white uniforms. Color was stripped from my life, but that wasn't all. I was stripped of movement. Paralyzed, the doctors said, from my neck down. It was a C 5/6 separation.

Whatever that meant.

I couldn't move. Alcohol, the very poison that had crippled my relationships and contributed to the destruction of my marriage, paralyzed my body and dramatically and irreversibly changed me. The intact, fully functioning person I'd always been no longer existed.

Before dinner that night, I was independent and self-reliant. I'd been revitalized and had finally found happiness and direction, purpose and a renewed sense of well-being. But after dinner that night, I was physiologically torn in two and radically and irreparably changed. My mind would never connect with my body again. They were completely severed, and communication between them was forever silenced. Their relationship was lost.

For twenty-eight years I'd been able to control myself and my movements, and in a moment it was gone. The drunk driver who was out of control of himself and his car had turned the tables. Now it was my life that was out of control. I tried to convince myself that this nightmare would go away or last only a few days, and that life as I'd always known it would resume. I kept telling myself that this wasn't permanent. It wasn't going to last forever.

But in the meantime, in those first days and hours, I had to cope. And I didn't know how.

Then, one day Dad brought an attorney to my hospital room for me to sign all my affairs over to him. Someone placed a pen in my limp and crooked hand and held a clipboard with the legal papers attached. I managed to scribble an X on the dotted line. No name. No life. No going back. No more being me.

This drastic swing of the pendulum from self-sufficiency to absolute dependency left me more desperate and afraid than I can describe. Everything about my life, about me, was unfamiliar.

I was lost.

The Beginning of an End

*Have you ever felt like you were a one-man army fight-
ing the whole world? Do you remember when you
finally gave in and waved a white flag of surrender?
Did you feel like a failure, or did you feel a
sense of relief on the horizon?*

Mark moved into my home to care for my property and my animals, and he assumed my position at the gift shop. Maureen and her husband, Don, welcomed my girls into their home to live with them and their children in Santa Barbara, California. But as life started to fall into place for others, mine continued to fall apart. My grief for the old Margaret and my old life relentlessly intensified until some-time, somehow, it gradually gave way and the slow process of dying to my old life began.

I had so many conflicting emotions. I was glad to be alive, and I desperately wanted another chance in life. I ached to care for my girls and be a better mom, and I longed to be capable of being more loving to all people. But I hated my existence. My life was as bland and sterile as my surroundings, and I yearned for color to come back into my life. I wanted my mind-body relationship restored so life as I'd always known it could be restored as well.

The fact that there was no color, no movement, and no life that I understood dominated my thoughts. The hours ahead unfolded the reality of my losses. I couldn't walk, run, jump, dance, climb, reach, grasp, squeeze, hug, roll over, or sit up. I couldn't control my bowels, urinate, feed myself, or wipe away a tear. I had lost my dignity, my looks, my pride, and my privacy. I couldn't be a mother to Julie and Jolene. I couldn't care for their needs or be there for them. I couldn't work to provide for myself and my girls.

And that wasn't all.

My hospital bed was now my home. It was fully furnished with straps, a neck brace, and tong traction (screws drilled into the sides of my head with ropes attached and weights hanging from them to keep my neck and body perfectly still). The only way for me to exist now was for others to be my hands, my legs, and my arms and for others to pick up all the pieces of my life and carry them. I was overwhelmed with sadness and fear. So much loss, so suddenly thrust upon me, was unbearable. I'd been invaded. All that once had been private and secret was openly exposed for everyone to see. I was embarrassed and humiliated. I became numb, and as a turtle cowers within its shell, I coveted protection and escape—anything to ward off this pain. This endless suffering. This soul-shattering loss.

Strangely, I wasn't angry with the drunk driver. I assumed my torment was deserved and the penalty of my bad behavior. I thought I was being punished for my sins of divorce, immorality, and drugs.

I shouldn't have been born. I was a mistake played in my mind. I had to physically work to be useful, but my arms and legs were useless. I had to be pretty to be successful, but my bumps and bruises and disabilities had left me far from attractive.

A crushing weight of guilt and shame hung over me, but somewhere in the midst of all these emotions, a very different life was gently being born.

I didn't know if this was the beginning of an end, or the end before a new beginning. The only thing I knew for sure was that my body was physically useless and my mind and soul were too troubled to function rationally. I couldn't make sense of anything, and thoughts about my future were more frightening than I can describe.

The Patient

Have you ever suffered an illness or incapacitation
(physical, mental, or emotional) that demanded that oth-
ers care for you and make decisions on your behalf?
Has anyone ever encouraged you to remain hopeful
when all hope seemed to vanish? Has someone
you didn't know ever surprised you with
extraordinary and unsolicited help?

As a patient in the intensive care unit at Marion Hospital, I received complete, around-the-clock care. The nurses were highly skilled and genuinely compassionate. Although I was totally helpless, I felt safe. And although I was totally dependent and utterly powerless to care for myself, I felt secure.

I spent five days in the ICU enduring an endless string of X-rays, needles, therapy, and tong traction. Doctors came by every few hours to see if I could move my toes. In addition to my spinal cord injury, I had a broken thumb (which hurt more than anything else) and a concussion on my forehead. Each day seemed to trickle into the next with the various treatments. I typically let the doctors and other medical staff members do with me as they pleased, but when they were about to shave my entire head because of the concussion, I was upset. To my surprise, a nurse came to my rescue and suggested they shave just the necessary area. Vanity still reigned!

I had physical therapy treatments every couple of hours to keep my body from deteriorating. My therapist helped me understand what was happening to me and patiently answered all my questions. I was so naïve. I didn't know what a spinal cord was or how it affected me.

I had no idea how long my recovery would take or if I would recover at all. I didn't know if I should even hope to walk again.

Fortunately, my therapist explained everything to me without using a lot of medical terminology that was over my head. He compared my injury to a lamp. My brain was the lightbulb, my spinal cord was the electrical cord, and the plug was my body. The cord was only partially severed, so a tiny current still flowed from my brain to my body. Because of this tiny current, I felt some sensations such as touch and pressure, and I was aware of my body at all times. From my chest down, I felt some levels of pain, but I wasn't able to feel hot or cold. I learned that some of my nerve damage would ultimately heal and some would not. Only time would tell. He said he hoped there would be a cure someday for spinal cord injuries, and he encouraged me to hold on to that hope no matter what.

Then he impressed upon me that I must be aware of my surroundings and make my needs known. This gentle man was a godsend who protected me, encouraged me, and educated me. I thank God for him still and wonder how I'd have survived without his tender care.

The day the doctors announced they were certain that I was going to live, Mom burst into tears. She'd had no idea that I might not. The first day my aunt visited, she left my room in shock and fainted in the hallway. That was the day I asked for a mirror—and I was shocked myself. No wonder she fainted! It wasn't me. The image I saw was pale and swollen with a half-shaven head. Seeing my reflection in that mirror initiated another bout of wondering where I was, and who I had become. It was bizarre, like some kind of amnesia. Nevertheless, since all I could control was my mind, I determined to be strong, courageous, and hopeful.

When I was eventually moved out of critical care and into the general ward, I thought I'd entered a carnival. There were so many things going on, it didn't seem as if anyone was in control, or cared, or even knew what they were doing.

That was when I learned the reality of my therapist's warning to stay alert and be vocal.

All day, every day, I lay on my back hooked up to an array of apparatuses. I couldn't do anything myself. Although the thought of me feeding myself was absurd, the first meal I received was plopped down on my hospital tray and left there. I could smell the food, but I couldn't get to it. I was helpless, humiliated, and hungry!

My next meal was served with orders for the nurse to stay and feed me. I'll never forget her. The first thing she said was, "Honey, let's sit you up to eat your meal." It was time to take control of the situation. From that point on, my family and friends came at mealtime to feed me. Different ones came for breakfast and lunch, but Marv always came for my evening meal.

Even though my head and neck were in traction, it was still necessary to refrain from any movement, so I couldn't get my hair shampooed, and I couldn't reach up to scratch my itchy head. There were still dried blood and bits of glass from the accident embedded in my scalp. Relief from itching was impossible and it drove me crazy. Something so tiny was unbearable. One night it was so overwhelming I just cried. One of the nurses heard me and came to my rescue. She stopped all her busy duties and attended to my needs. She brought in some baby oil and Q-tips and began gently rubbing my head with them. As she did, she quietly sang some old gospel hymns. Her simple gesture brought me amazing comfort and relief, and the rest of my night was more peaceful.

I was amazed at the strong support that surrounded me. I had so many visitors and received so many cards that I couldn't count them, and I received so many bouquets of flowers that I shared them with other patients. And right in the middle of all those beautiful gifts and precious people was Marv. When New Year's Eve rolled around, toting two margaritas, confetti, and balloons, Marv snuck up to see me at midnight to celebrate. The night of my accident we'd made a date, and he wasn't about to let me down.

After three weeks in Marion Hospital, the doctors sent me to a rehabilitation facility in Santa Barbara where I could receive more therapy and continue the slow process of mending my broken body. Prior to my departure the nurses shampooed my hair as my going-away present. It was messy and awkward, but oh so heavenly.

The drive from Santa Maria to Santa Barbara follows California's beautiful coastline, and I was looking forward to taking in every speck of it. After so much time in the hospital spent staring at white walls, the breathtaking cliffs and the Pacific Ocean would be a sight for very sore eyes. I couldn't wait to get in that ambulance!

Unfortunately, my ambulance didn't have windows. I was a little deflated, but I convinced myself that it wasn't that big of a deal because it was, after all, only an hour-long drive. Little did I know that my ambulance driver was instructed to not exceed twenty miles per hour. Ultimately the typically easy, scenic, one-hour drive ballooned into a tedious three-hour marathon. Fortunately, Marv was with me for company and encouragement, but when we finally arrived, I couldn't wait to get out of that ambulance!

And when I was out and wheeled toward the facility, one of the first things I noticed was a sign above the door that read: *Hope renewed, Faith restored.*

My heart needed hope more than anything at this point. I was optimistic, encouraged, and eager.

Unbearable

*What prisons have you encountered in your life? What
has held or continues to hold you captive? Has anyone
ever used their power or authority to take unfair
advantage of you? Has anyone stood by your
side who didn't have to?*

The sign above the entryway at the rehab facility was reassuring,
but before any renewed hope or restored faith could apply
to me, I needed more X-rays. And sadly those X-rays revealed that
my injury hadn't healed enough for me to qualify for a wheelchair.
Instead, I was introduced to something called a Stryker bed.

I was placed flat on my back on what looked like an oversized
ironing board with one person standing on each side of me. Immediately, they started calling out orders.

"Board in place."

"Check."

"Strap on forehead."

"Check."

"Strap on shoulders."

"Check."

And on it went to my waist, my knees, and my feet. The orders
flew back and forth from one to the other.

"Now turn."

In just seconds, I was facedown staring at the white floor and the
two mysterious people were gone. I was still, as death is still. I'd had

no choice in my treatment. I was trapped and terrified of the unknown. Then, three hours later, the two mystery people returned, assumed their places on each side of me, and started barking orders again.

"Board in place."..."Check straps."... "One. Two. Three. Turn." The world spun around, and I lay faceup staring at the ceiling again. Then, "Remove board. Loosen straps." The orders went on. Since I wore a neck brace, I couldn't look from side to side so I stared either at a white ceiling or a white floor. I didn't know if this was prison, torture, or hell.

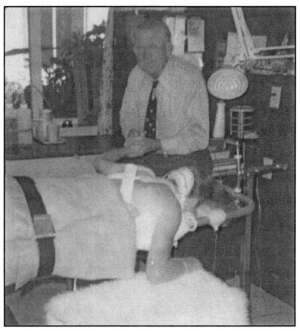

1976, Prone on the Stryker Bed

I was exhausted and hungry after the long drive to Santa Barbara. I'd been exposed to new surroundings, different doctors and nurses, more X-rays, and the nightmare called a Stryker bed. It was overwhelming. Finally, about 9 P.M. a nurse arrived with my dinner. But when she took the lid off and we saw that it was spaghetti, which is impossible to eat lying down, we both had to laugh. And then I cried. She was so patient and kind. As she fed me, tears flowed down my cheeks, and she silently wiped them away. She didn't ask any questions. She was just there, and I sensed her compassion for me.

Not long after she left an unusual-looking man rolled into my room in his wheelchair and offered to share his bottle of liquor with me. I was tempted to drown my sorrows and grief, but I couldn't. I couldn't hold a glass or a bottle by myself.

That was my first day and night in the facility that touted: *Hope renewed, Faith restored.*

The orders were unyielding. I was the patient, orders came from the neurologist, and nurses carried them out. It was the same battery of orders every three hours, twenty-four hours every day, for two months. I was confined, oppressed, and subject to this monstrous bed and those who operated it. My body was continually manipulated and manhandled.

Every room had eight patients. Every patient had six doctors, one RN, and several nurse's aides, so solitude and privacy were nonexistent. I desperately needed some time by myself, and I longed to go outside, but leaving was impossible unless someone was available to push me. If I could get outside, I thought, I'd be able to see the sky—or the ground—depending on my Stryker bed schedule.

It didn't take long for me to become familiar with the different nurses and their respective shifts. The night shift was scary. Those nurses seemed angry just to be awake.

One night the charge nurse (known as "the General") announced that she was going to turn me by herself. The problem was that I knew the first rule in Stryker-bed operation was: it takes two to flip; and two to flop. A partner was always necessary. I was petrified, but when I challenged her, she said that she'd done this so many times she could do it blindfolded.

I screamed and woke everyone up, but since everyone in my room was paralyzed, too, they couldn't help me. "The General" turned me over anyway, but she forgot to strap down my head and it jerked. I was sure my injury had worsened. The following morning I nervously told the head nurse what happened. I knew this was a dangerous thing to do because if "the General" found out that I'd reported her, she could take revenge the next night. The odds were against me. When disputes occurred, the nurses were typically trusted rather than the patients. But I had to protect myself, so I submitted a report, and incredibly, so did all my roommates. They, too, risked everything by speaking up on my behalf.

I was shocked when the verdict was in my favor. "The General" was ordered to always have a partner when she turned me, but the best part was that she was much nicer to me from then on.

Those early days of Stryker-bed therapy were gruesome. If it hadn't been for my family, I don't know how I'd have managed to maintain my sanity. Maureen brought my girls to see me every day. They'd crawl on the floor under my bed when I was facedown so we could do their homework together. Friday nights were always special because Maureen brought dinner and her children as well as mine for a feast. Then on Sundays, my folks would visit and bring BBQ dinners for everyone in the ward. All these wonderfully generous efforts kept me connected to life outside the hospital.

Hope Renewed

Do you recall an inner sense of hope during or immediately following a particular struggle? Has anyone ever tried to take your hope away? Do you think you've ever been visited by an angel?

From the moment of my injury, and in spite of continuous challenges, setbacks, and incredible bouts of frustration and sadness, I somehow maintained hope in my heart that everything would be okay. Linked to my hope was an expectation of change. My hope assured me this crushing, painful time would ultimately pass. I clung to the rehab's promise of, *"Hope renewed and Faith restored."*

Hope gave me life and carried me through the long, lonely days and nights of separation from my girls and my family, my home, my workplace, and everyone and everything I loved and lost. Hope carried me through the awkwardness of having others care for my body and the details of my life. Hope gave me courage to live another day, to smile and laugh, and to cherish all the love and support that surrounded me.

The hope I developed was through sheer determination, so when I was told that part of my therapy was psychological counseling, I was both anxious and nervous. Unfortunately, my first appointment happened to fall when I was facedown in my Stryker bed. I was wheeled into the counselor's office, and as he introduced himself all I remember is staring at his sandals and hairy toes. I felt like a piece of furniture or an object, a robot, or a machine.

Then he asked me if I'd accepted the fact that I'd never walk again, and that I'd always be in a wheelchair. I was shocked. I told him that I hadn't accepted any such fact, and I remained hopeful that I'd walk again. But that wasn't the answer he was looking for. He told me that I couldn't leave the facility until I accepted my paralysis, and that I had better start accepting it immediately.

I stood my ground and insisted that he'd best not try to take my hope away because that was all I had. He said it was false hope. And that was the end of the appointment.

After that, an unbearably dark cloud and heaviness bore down on me. A massive door had been slammed in my face and on my heart. And although I'd boasted that nothing and no one could take my hope away, it vanished. I was consumed by despair and the dread of being eternally helpless and bound to this insufferable disability. I didn't want to see anyone. I canceled all my therapy—especially with that counselor. I never wanted to see him or his hairy toes again. I withdrew into a dark world of hopelessness. Thoughts of suicide arose. I desperately wanted to end this existence, but I was physically unable to do even that. The only future I imagined was fraught with helplessness and total dependency. I had to be fed, bathed, dressed, pushed, and rolled over, and I didn't want to live that way.

Hope was critical to my healing process. I needed it to keep me motivated and looking forward to tomorrow, but it was taken from me. And without it, living seemed pointless.

One day as I was lying outside in the Stryker bed staring at the blue sky, doing my best to escape into nothingness, a man approached me and said that I was lying in his bed. That sounded outrageous because he was obviously standing beside me. Then he explained that some of his loneliest moments were in a Stryker bed but he'd been healed. He advised me to not allow anyone, not therapist or doctor or nurse, to destroy my hope of walking again. He said there was always hope.

Immediately, the massive weight of despair lifted. It just took those few words of encouragement to free me to believe again in a hope-filled, healthy future. Then he gave me a mirror with a movable arm on it that could be attached to my bed so I could see people when I was prone. He knew the loneliness and isolation that was synonymous with Stryker-bed constraint. I never saw him again, but his visit renewed my hope. Maybe he was an angel of God. Whoever he was, I'll never forget him.

After two months of Stryker-bed traction, it was time for X-rays to see if my neck had healed. I was so anxious to get up and move around, even if it was only in a wheelchair. I waited in line all day for X-rays, but the lab closed before it was my turn. My nurse was furious and made certain I was first on the schedule the next morning.

When I arrived, the room was cold and completely furnished in stainless steel. I was lifted out of bed, propped up on a table, and instructed to be very still. I was not to move. My neck brace was slowly and gently removed, and I was reminded again, "Do not move your neck."

Then someone dropped an X-ray tray. The loud noise startled me, and I flinched. It felt as if my head was about to fall off, and I burst into tears. I was certain I'd ruined all these months in traction. But I was wrong. My X-rays showed that my bones were completely healed, and I could bid farewell to the Stryker bed and my neck brace.

It was wonderful to be out of that contraption. It was a huge step in my physical healing, and I was eager for the next step. And I was also eager to be able to sit up so I could see the faces that belonged to the voices of the friends I'd made in my ward.

Change of Heart

*Has someone or something come into your life that
caused you to have a change of heart? Have you had
to rethink some opinions or judgments because
you were in a time or place that gave you an
entirely different outlook?*

In spite of the horrors of the Stryker bed, the fiasco with "the General," and the lack of hope or empathy from the psychologist, moving to the rehab facility was unquestionably a step in the right direction for my restoration. But it was also a frightening step. I'd never been around disabled people before. I didn't know if they'd be normal, or insane, or scary looking, and I didn't know how to overcome my fear. Everything and everyone in my new world was unfamiliar and strange. I'd only seen the ceiling and the floor and a few feet and some wheelchair wheels as they passed by.

The only faces I'd seen were those that peered directly over me, or those that lay on the floor directly underneath me. And the only voices I recognized belonged to those few patients who wheeled next to me and shared their stories so that I could share mine. The amazing thing was that sharing our lives, our hurts, and our hearts before we even made eye contact made our times together even more precious. It was impossible for me to judge them by their appearance. They were just people, real people with real feelings, and they were beautiful. I knew their laughter, shared their tears, and understood their pain. They were just like me—normal and ordinary. They were just like me—trapped in their bodies trying desperately to make it through one more day. They were my friends, and I treasured them.

As time marched on and our relationships deepened, I longed to see them. I loved them, and I didn't care how they looked. I'd had a change of heart. All my fears and concerns vanished. Love and acceptance had overcome them.

Now that I was done with the Stryker bed, I thought I would finally be able connect the hearts and voices that I'd grown to love with their faces. But it wasn't meant to be just yet.

Since the X-rays showed that my neck bones had healed adequately, the next step in restoring my body included something called a tilt table. For a couple of hours each day, I was taken to a separate room, wrapped from my chest to my ankles in Ace bandages, and placed on this new contraption that inclined me at varying angles. After lying flat for so many months, my circulation was limited, and my body needed to slowly get used to the pressure of being upright. For ten days the tilt table was gradually slanted to more upright positions. When I wasn't on the tilt table, I was still lying flat in my hospital bed.

After I completed the tilt table therapy, my next big challenge was sitting up. I'd been lying down for three months so this was a great reason to celebrate! All those voices that had cried in shared disappointments, frustrations, and fears, and laughed in mutual encouragement and support, surrounded me and waited almost breathlessly as my caretaker pushed the button allowing my slow and squeaky electric bed to sit me upright. We were all excited, and my heart pounded in anticipation.

I could finally see the gold and the glitter in the faces of my newfound treasure chest of friends, and they were beautiful. Each and every one sparkled, inside and out. This one brief encounter was so instrumental in energizing me. Seeing them and connecting with them on another level gave me strength when everything else was such a huge struggle and seemed to take such a long time.

I went to therapy every hour and worked to strengthen my atrophied muscles. It was incredibly difficult and ever so slow. Even picking up a small block seemed like an impossible task. It was so humiliating to think that I was twenty-eight years old and had to learn once again how to sit up and pick up objects. There were times when I thought I just couldn't persevere one more minute. And then one day I wrote my name. I'll never forget it. I'd found a long-lost critical piece of my past, and I was greatly encouraged.

Since I was anxious to go home and be a mom for my girls again, I had to learn how to cook from my wheelchair. I had to learn how to open a refrigerator door while parked in front of it. I had to learn how to break an egg with disabled fingers and how to open containers. There were so many things I had to learn that I'd always taken for granted. Yet incredibly, laughter seemed to replace my tears and a new life seemed to be defeating what had felt so much like death.

After several weeks of kitchen training and practice, I cooked an entire dinner on my own in the kitchen of the rehab center and invited Marv to share it with me. I was so excited. When he arrived I couldn't wait to show him what I'd accomplished. But when we went into the kitchen, we discovered that some unknown sneaky Little Red Riding Hood had eaten every bit of it! I was devastated and terribly disappointed. There was no privacy. I had to get out of there.

I requested some type of solitude. Even an hour of retreat would have been such a relief. After some pleading, my caretakers relented and allowed me to visit a beautiful garden in a separate building. Sixty minutes of uninterrupted silence. Peace at last. It was wonderful ... until I eventually realized they'd forgotten about me. The nurse who'd escorted me out had gone off duty and neglected to tell her replacement where I was. I was stuck. I couldn't get out of the garden because there were steps, and I couldn't reach the phone. I yelled, but no one heard me.

It wasn't until the night shift came on duty that someone noticed I was missing and searched for me and found me. So much for my hour of serenity.

Even though my family and friends and acquaintances remained immensely devoted to me with visits and gifts, depression lurked. Even though so many people did so much to keep me optimistic and upbeat, despair was always just a blink away. Some girlfriends even made me a quilt that said, "We Love You." It was amazing and so loving, but grief always trumped any other emotion—grief for the loss of my healthy body and grief for each of the eight girls in my room. Each one died. And each one was a profound loss.

Then one day Maureen told me that it was my outlook that dictated the outlook of others. I was so surprised. If I was down or depressed, she said, then everyone who visited me would feel the same. She told me that I was the one who held everyone together, and she suggested that I "just be happy"!

I tried to "just be happy" on the outside, but it didn't match what I was feeling on the inside.

Love Never Fails

*Is there someone in your life who loves you beyond what
seems rational? Have you ever followed your heart in
love even though the odds were against you? Have you
ever heard God speak to you loud and clear and
followed His direction without stopping to analyze
and rationalize all the pros and cons?*

After my accident, Marv and I made a list of the potential positives and negatives in our relationship. The negatives were my disability, my life in a wheelchair, my total dependence on others to be my legs and arms and fingers, and all the other things that remained unknown. Marv had been a bachelor for ten years. We'd both been divorced. He had four adult children. I had two young girls. I had five acres and a yard full of animals to maintain, and Marv had a modest salary from the dive shop. Everything seemed to be against us.

Since the only thing on the positive side of our list was that we loved each other, we were too afraid to pursue our relationship. Our list made it clear that the odds were definitely against us, but as it turned out, following the odds wasn't in the cards.

About eight o'clock one evening, while I was still hospitalized in the Santa Barbara rehab facility, I was lying in my bed and feeling really downhearted as I pondered my life and my future. I longed for some answers and direction, but as far as I could see, there was nothing positive ahead. Everything looked terribly grim.

And then Marv popped in with an unexpected visit.

He walked over to me and said, "I'm yours." I didn't understand. We'd just listed all the reasons why our relationship wouldn't work. Then he repeated himself: "I'm yours. I'm here to tell you, I'm yours. You can marry me, rent me, or live with me. Whatever. I'm yours, and I'm not going to leave your side." With that, he fell on my bed and we hugged, cried, and laughed with joy.

Then he told me that he'd been sitting at home when he heard a voice tell him to come to me and tell me that he belonged with me and wouldn't leave my side. He said it was a powerful, direct, and clear order from the Most High God! I didn't know how to receive so much love—a love so great it wouldn't allow life's difficulties or tragedies or circumstances to deteriorate it or divide us, a love so strong it would shelter our weakest moments and shatter our ugliest ones, a love so vast it would still our most frightening encounters, a love so committed it would never fail.

A Mother's Heart

*If you're a parent, think of your children. If not, think of
your parents. As a family, do you pull together to make
your home happy regardless of finances and obstacles?
Is being together what matters most?*

My six months of bizarre contraptions, endless physical therapy, and unimaginable emotions were finally over. I could go home.

Marv faithfully stayed by my side. Having my girls with me again was more precious than I can describe. I had an attendant stay with me during the day, and Marv was with me at night. The attendant bathed me, dressed me, cooked our meals, did the laundry, and taxied the girls to and from school. She ran the house, and I watched. I was thankful to be home, but I was incapable of doing most of the work that I'd always so enjoyed. I no longer knew my purpose or my role. I desperately wanted my old life back.

Government social services provided the attendant and contributed my monthly income, so they were obligated to keep a close watch on our home life. After one of their evaluations, they determined that my home was an unsafe environment, I was an unfit mother, and I was unable to properly care for my girls.

Marv and I were angry, frightened, and brokenhearted. No government agency should have that much control of our lives. We certainly needed their stipend and the attendant, but we didn't need them to judge our family life. I couldn't meet all my girls' needs myself, but between the attendant and Marv, they were well cared for. I was terrified that my girls could be taken from me. Just being away from them while I was recuperating had been heart-wrenching.

Then precisely as I'd vowed to be a better daughter, I vowed to be a better mother. I would be there for them, care for them, nurture, and teach them. I wanted to enjoy them, laugh and cry with them, and encourage and support them in everything. After nearly losing my life, life had taken on a whole new dimension. Before my accident, my career and my needs typically came first. Now, nothing was more important than my daughters.

At rehab, I'd learned how to shop for handicap-friendly appliances and kitchen tools, how to open doors and jars, and how to reach for objects and plug cords into sockets. But my goal never changed: I wanted to be a mom again. I needed my girls, and they needed me.

That poor evaluation caused us to pull together as a family and make some important decisions. It was a huge step of faith, but if we were going to be a family, we had to discontinue our dependence on everything the social services provided.

We cut back as much as possible on all our expenses. Julie and Jolene assumed a lot more of our domestic chores. We turned up the volume on our favorite music and sang as we cleaned, cooked, and vacuumed. Meals became a fun time of instructing and laughing our way through spills. We hired a part-time girl, Heidi, to help me in the morning with my personal needs. We were all together and that was what mattered. I was there for Julie and Jolene, teaching them, cheering them on, and loving them. I was thankful for them every moment, and every moment was a blessing.

Many years later, when Julie was working at the jewelry store with Mark, the social worker who'd given us the bad report came in to browse. She was amazed at the lovely young woman Julie had become and wrote me a note of apology commending us on our parenting skills. She explained that we had been her first case, and she hadn't understood the importance of looking at the entire family unit.

Today, my girls are married, raising their own families, and making beautiful, positive contributions to this world. They love God and their husbands, and they cherish the privilege of raising their own children.

A mother's heart won.

Our Wedding Day

Is your spouse the one who completes you or competes with you? In retrospect, was the focus of your wedding an intimate celebration of two lives becoming one or something more superficial? Have you experienced the reality that marriage is much more than just living together?

Marv and I lived together for a year, and then he decided that something just wasn't right. So on July 24, 1977, while sitting on a swing covered in beautiful flowers in the midst of our garden, we were married. I was barefoot and wore a flowered dress. I felt so complete with Marv by my side. Julie and Jolene were our flower girls, and Maureen's children rang the bells to start the ceremony. Our guests witnessed our vows sitting on bales of hay. It was a simple and intimate wedding. We loved and laughed and celebrated life. Our two souls and hearts were made one by God. Marv and I, friends and lovers, were entwined together for life's journey.

For a year we'd been a family of four. After we got married, we were still a family of four, but there was a difference. There was something more, something intangible. The mother's heart I'd hoped for and dreamed of for so many years was even more genuine and more prized.

July 24, 1977
Two hearts joined by God

Our new family of four
Julie, me, Marv, Jolene

Broken ...

*Have you ever thought that life was just not worth the
pain, the heartache, and the disappointment that it
brings? Have you ever been in a situation when you
thought life couldn't be more heart-wrenching—and
then it was? How did you respond? Where did
you find your answer?*

Life eased into a daily rhythm. In the mornings Marv left for work,
the girls left for school, and Heidi came to help me. She was
a sweet young Christian who loved Jesus. She repeatedly invited me to
church, and I repeatedly refused her invitation. I didn't need church.
My neighbor Sheila was also a sweet Christian woman who frequently
invited me to her home for a group Bible study. But I always declined
her invitation because I didn't need Bible study.

I was still struggling with defining my purpose and my goals, but
I didn't think anyone else could help or relate to my special circumstances. I didn't know what value I had, if any. I believed everything
hinged on doing good deeds for others. But I couldn't do any good
deeds. I couldn't do anything. I craved the ability to contribute to
my life and the lives of others by doing, fixing, and giving. But all I
could manage was sitting and watching while others went through
those motions.

I remained convinced that my appearance defined me, and my
appearance was quickly transforming from attractive to disabled and
awkward. People stared. They seemed mesmerized by my wheelchair.
I hated going out in public, and yet I longed to go back to work. I

missed decorating windows and buying and selling inventory at the gift shop. But that door was closed. My codependency kept resurfacing. Just as I strove to fix and please Mom, I wanted to fix and please others. I wanted to make others happy, but it was impossible because I was unhappy, lonely, and lost. Shame and self-hatred prevailed. I berated myself for being such a problem to everyone. I was crumbling. I was just a mistake—again.

The days just rolled on.

And then another crushing blow.

It was Thanksgiving Day, 1977, not quite two years after my accident. Family members from near and far were gathering at Mom and Dad's to celebrate and feast on lots of yummy food. The weather was picture-perfect, and everyone was excited. Maureen and her family were driving up from Santa Barbara. I was really looking forward to seeing them, but when Marv, the girls and I pulled into the driveway, Dad greeted us and said there'd been an accident.

"Jesus," was all I could mutter.

A brand-new tire had blown out and flipped their car. Maureen and her husband, Don, were critically injured. Their five-year-old son, Donald, was dead. Their seven-year-old daughter, Melby Lynn, was on life support, and she survived just long enough for Dad to see her. No other cars were involved.

I was shocked. This couldn't be happening. I'd already endured so much pain in my life. I remember being thankful that Maureen's children were spared the pain and loss that life brings, but the agony we experienced from losing their sweet lives was staggering. Our grief was so intense that just taking a breath was excruciating. Dinner was never served. Everyone scattered to try to assimilate what was happening. Tears, unbelief, and fear gripped us.

Maureen and Don's bodies would heal, but not their hearts. Their family was crushed and couldn't be put back together again. It was devastating to witness their pain. Life hurt. It was so unfair. First my body was broken. Now my family was broken. This anguish, loss, and heartache led me on a desperate search to find some comfort, some peace, some answers to life.

I wondered *why* all this was happening, but more than that, I wondered *what* was happening. Everything was out of control. It was as if life was a bag of marbles spilled across the floor, and I needed to gather them up in one swoop, but I couldn't. Could life just be a series of catastrophes? How and where could I find peace in the midst of so much heartache?

Finally I said "yes" when Heidi invited me to church, and I said "yes" when Sheila invited me to Bible study. Now I was surrounded with people who loved Jesus, and they gently led me to the foot of the cross ... the beautiful, rugged cross. I was desperately broken.

I began to hear the truth of God's Word.

> *Jesus said to him, "I am the way, and the truth, and the life.*
> *No one comes to the Father except through me."*
> —John 14:6

His truth began to define me and replace the lies that had previously guided me. I was on the threshold of finding purpose and meaning in my life.

> *and you will know the truth, and the truth will set you free.*
> —John 8:32

Freedom was coming as I discovered God's amazing grace, His unconditional acceptance, and His unfathomable forgiveness.

> *For by grace you have been saved through faith. And this*
> *is not your own doing; it is the gift of God.*
> —Ephesians 2:8

At last I'd found unwavering comfort and unexplainable peace. At last, I knew what it meant to be saved, to be born again.

> *For the Son of Man came to seek and to save the lost.*
> —Luke 19:10

At last I knew what if felt like to be found, and I understood what God truly desired from me.

> The sacrifices of God are a broken spirit; a broken and contrite heart, O God, you will not despise.
>
> —Psalm 51:17

... and Beautiful

When did you first experience the difference that Jesus makes in your life? Whom did God use to draw you to Him? Do you remember the joy and the freedom you experienced those first days and months as a born-again Christian? Do you still rest in Jesus' strength and wisdom and simultaneously yearn for more?

Now, instead of trying to hold on to life in my own strength and make sense of it in my own wisdom, I could hold on tight to Jesus and allow Him to be my strength and my wisdom. Now, I held tight to all the precious people in my life. They became special gifts from God to be opened and enjoyed for as long as I was alive.

Healing and salvation also came to Julie and Jolene, and the three of us were baptized in the name of Jesus in May 1980. Marv got into the pool of water with me for my immersion because he didn't trust anyone else to hold me. And after my baptism was finished, Mom got the tricky task of pulling off my wet jeans. We laughed so hysterically in the process that she nearly lost her strength altogether!

The pastor of the church I attended preached straight from the Bible. I learned so much truth about the love of Christ. I was beginning to be set free from the lies that had bound me all my life.

I wasn't the cause of Mom's drinking; it was just a result of living in a fallen world. No one escapes feeling hurt or broken in some way; some just manage to cover it up better than others.

All we like sheep have gone astray; we have turned—every one—to his own way;

—Isaiah 53:6

It wasn't my outward appearance that mattered to God; it was inner beauty that pleased Him. That was really exciting, because it was something I could achieve.

Do not let your adorning be external—the braiding of hair and the putting on of gold jewelry, or the clothing you wear—but let your adorning be the hidden person of the heart with the imperishable beauty of a gentle and quiet spirit, which in God's sight is very precious.

—1 Peter 3:3–4

I wasn't a mistake; I was part of God's plan from the beginning of time.

I praise you, for I am fearfully and wonderfully made. Wonderful are your works; my soul knows it very well. My frame was not hidden from you, when I was being made in secret, intricately woven in the depths of the earth. Your eyes saw my unformed substance; in your book were written, every one of them, the days that were formed for me, when as yet there were none of them. How precious to me are your thoughts, O God! How vast is the sum of them!

—Psalm 139:14–17

And it wasn't good works that saved me; it was God's grace. I just needed to embrace the gift of grace and be a child of God. What freedom from works!

He saved us, not because of works done by us in righteousness, but according to his own mercy, by the washing of

regeneration and renewal of the Holy Spirit, whom he
poured out on us richly through Jesus Christ our Savior.
—Titus 3:5–6

I began to see and understand that life has many problems, but I was not always the cause of every problem. God's forgiveness set me free from guilt and shame. My purpose now was to be like Jesus, to know Him, and to bring Him glory. A hunger and thirst came into my spirit, and my journey with Jesus as Lord began.

One of the first things the Holy Spirit prompted me to do was to write a letter to Mom and Dad and ask for their forgiveness. I'd wrongfully counted on them to fix and change all that was broken in my life, and I'd depended on them for things that God alone was able to provide. I finally understood that the acceptance and unconditional love I'd hungered for could be found only in Almighty God. It finally sank in that, although honoring my parents was of utmost importance, God was, first and foremost, the One I must seek to please.

In my letter I thanked Mom and Dad for all the love and provision and care they'd given me throughout my life. They had been a beautiful shadow of who ultimately filled my heart. At last I could say without reservation that God's amazing presence lived within me and filled the deep hole that had been in my heart for so many years.

Forgiveness set everyone free.

Bible study classes at Sheila's changed my old life into one that was fresh and new. These were some of my best times. I was growing in God's Word and developing precious relationships with others who loved the Lord as I did. I met some of my dearest friends—Jeanie, Sheila, Vicki, and Debra—at Bible study and church.

It had taken years. It had taken catastrophe. It had taken unbelievable sorrow and loss. But it was all worth it to finally see the Way—not the way of good works, idols, hollow religion, and reciting mantras—but the Way to peace and life everlasting in the very presence of Jesus in heaven. If it meant all the pain and heartache of past failures and mistakes to understand the truth that I am a sinner in need of a Savior—a Savior who gives the perfect gifts of forgiveness and grace—then the price was not too great.

If you confess with your mouth that Jesus is Lord and believe in your heart that God raised him from the dead, you will be saved. For with the heart one believes and is justified, and with the mouth one confesses and is saved.

—Romans 10:9–10

I'd been broken and now Jesus could make something beautiful of my life—of me.

The Offering Plate

What's the most humbling thing that's happened to you at church? Were you able to laugh at it?

Now that I'd become a child of God, I had purpose and value. Each new day overflowed with His grace. My circumstances hadn't changed, but I had. God had lifted me above them, and I was a product of His mighty work. In the midst of great difficulties, He'd radically changed my heart. Because of Jesus and by the power of the Holy Spirit, God filled me with heavenly peace and joy unlike any I'd ever known or attained on my own strength.

> *I know that you can do all things, and that no purpose of yours can be thwarted.*
>
> —Job 42:2

But although I'd begun receiving the incredible blessings of His love and forgiveness, I was still a beginner in figuring out how to live with my new physically compromised body. And interspersed among my newfound grace-filled moments were some very humbling ones.

Unfortunately, one that particularly stands out happened at a church gathering.

I remember looking forward to attending a James Dobson film with Jeanie. The church that was showing it was filled to capacity and the enthusiasm of the crowd was energetic and contagious. I didn't recognize many of the other people there, but that didn't matter. I parked my wheelchair at the end of one of the wooden pews, and Jeanie sat next to me.

The program was wonderful, and it was a special treat for us to have an evening out together. When the offering plate was passed during intermission, I immediately placed my twenty-dollar bill in it even though I'd planned to give only ten dollars. I knew I could quickly get change from the plate.

But God had a different plan. As I tried to retrieve my change, my fingers went into a spasm and gripped all the money in the plate. The more I tried to shake my hand open, the tighter my grip became. Jeanie elbowed me with a shocked expression and asked me what in the world I was doing! As I looked down the row, every head was turned and leaning out and watching me. I started to laugh (my natural reaction when I'm embarrassed) and begged Jeanie to help me open my hand. After she peeled open my fingers, the money fell into the plate, and she passed it on.

I just wanted change; I didn't want to make a spectacle of myself. I can't imagine what all those who witnessed my fiasco must have thought. Actually, I'm sure it's best that I don't know. But the bottom line is that I learned a very valuable lesson: never attempt to get change from the offering plate!

It was a very humbling and embarrassing experience, but it pales in comparison to another experience.

Swimming Drop-Out

When have you experienced something embarrassing
that brought unwanted attention to you? Can you laugh
at your shortcomings with friends, or do you get angry
and defensive?

I met Susan in a parking lot about a year after my accident. She was my age and a paraplegic as a result of an automobile accident that happened the same year as mine. It was such a blessing to meet someone whom I had so much in common with and who shared the same struggles and challenges associated with disabilities. We'd heard of an adaptive swim class that was offered at the junior college, so we decided to enroll. We were excited to embark on this adventure together. We imagined the fun we'd have exercising and the relief we'd feel to be free from our wheelchairs for a while. Jeanie came along and helped me change into and out of my swimsuit. (The water was cold, so I wore a short diver's wet suit. Thank goodness there weren't any hidden cameras recording the antics involved in getting me into it!)

The pool was filled with people with varying degrees of disabilities, and each one was assigned a personal attendant. After they lowered me into the water on the cranelike device, I met my attendant, Silas. He was a young student volunteer who was gentle, caring, and quiet-natured. I felt secure, and I trusted him with my life. All went well until my session ended, and Silas prepared to get me out of the pool.

We were facing each other as he brought me to the side of the pool and lifted me up and out and next to the crane. But as he sat me down, my legs jumped and stiffened. They were straight as boards and began to spasm violently and uncontrollably … right into Silas's crotch! He stood there with his eyes popping out as I just kept on kicking! I was speechless, and so was he. He eventually immersed himself into the water and disappeared in pain.

I was desperate to disappear, too. I was so embarrassed. I wanted God to "beam me up"—the sooner the better! Once that crane plopped me back into my wheelchair, I made a beeline to the locker room, where I found Jeanie and Susan laughing hysterically. That cold, foggy, miserable day was the first and last of my swimming classes. I don't know if it was Silas's first day, but it may have been his last!

> *A time for every matter under heaven … a time to weep,*
> *and a time to laugh; a time to mourn, and a time to dance.*
> —Ecclesiastes 3:1, 4

Getting Dressed

Do you tire of caring for others? Does your attitude re-
flect joy in being able and available to help, or do
you resent the inconvenience? Does your answer
reflect that you are dependent on yourself or God?

Routine tasks are so... routine! They're often meaningless, humdrum, and boring, and they can easily become rushed and sloppy, not just for the disabled, but for everyone. Still, the fact that I can't dress myself is the pits. My fingers can't zip, button, pull, or grab. Sitting in a chair trying to pull on a pair of pants without fully functioning hands is like trying to pull them up wearing boxing gloves. It's impossibly frustrating.

So dressing me is one of Marv's routine tasks, one that he's been doing for more than thirty years. It could understandably become tiresome for him and rushed through. And the inconvenience could easily contribute to a sour attitude.

Then one day, as I watched him, I was amazed at how careful he was. He took time to make sure everything was lined up, straight, and comfortable. He didn't hurry, and he wasn't anxious. He dressed me as he would dress himself. I had to know why he hadn't tired of this daily mundane obligation, and how he'd managed to do it with so much care and love and attention, so I asked him. But I wasn't prepared for his response.

He said that the day the Lord told him to be by my side and care for me he was given power to do just that. He said that same power was alive and well and hadn't diminished in time.

When God gives a task He also supplies the power and the divine gifts necessary to carry it out. Thank You, precious Lord, for Marv. He is my daily intimate, indispensable gift from God.

> *He who calls you is faithful; he will surely do it.*
> —1 Thessalonians 5:24

Miracles

*Close your eyes and think about all the tiny miracles
God has done throughout your life. Can you appreciate
the fact that nothing escapes His vision, He longs to meet
your needs, and He loves to surprise you with little bo-
nuses? Have there been times when you thought you were
totally alone and desperate but God was there all along
and longing to hold you and demonstrate His love?
Do you give Him credit in all circumstances
and crumble at His generosity?*

Previously unavailable power had entered me—the power of
God. He incrementally gave me more ability to accom-
plish more tasks. I was so grateful. I could wash and fold the laundry,
and cook meals and clean the kitchen. The more I sought Him first in
my life, even in the little things, the more He proved Himself faithful.

Each morning before everyone left for the day, I tried to think
through my schedule and determine what I might need that I couldn't
reach. (The Lord knew how to make me get organized!)

One day I was enjoying being home alone and thankful for the
things I could do. Marv and the girls had left. Stew was on the menu
for dinner that night, and Marv had put the Crock-Pot on the counter
for me and plugged it in. Right above my counter is a tall cabinet with
several shelves without doors that are lined with all our canned goods.
After I put the meat in the pot and added all the vegetables, I realized
I'd forgotten to have anyone retrieve the tomato sauce from the top
shelf. I was disappointed because I'd have to settle for adding just
water, and it wouldn't be nearly as tasty. There was nothing I could do

about it, though, so I wheeled around to the sink. As soon as I turned away, I heard a loud thud. And when I looked back, there was a can of tomato sauce sitting right next to the Crock-Pot! I couldn't believe my eyes. I couldn't believe that God cared enough about me to retrieve the tomato sauce for my stew. I couldn't believe that He would actually show me, with a can of tomato sauce, that He never leaves me.

I smiled and laughed, and I felt God's very real, very powerful presence. I saw firsthand how involved He is in the details of my life. When Marv and the girls came home and asked what was for dinner, I told them "miracle stew."

On another day, once again joyfully at home and conscious and thankful of all God's interventions and blessings, I was vacuuming. It was a challenging chore, but I liked the exercise, and I liked clean carpet! While I was in the girls' room, moving chairs to vacuum behind them, I lost my balance and fell to the floor. I couldn't move, and I had to pick the girls up from school in just forty-five minutes. I was angry and stuck.

I thought about dragging myself to the phone to call Marv, but he worked thirty minutes away, and I really didn't want to bother him. Besides, it was humiliating to have to be picked up off the floor. Then I thought I'd just pray that God would heal me and allow me to walk away from this humbling scenario. I immediately prayed. I asked God to raise me up if it was in line with His will and His timing. But I remained on the floor. Finally, I thought I'd pray for strength to pull myself back into my wheelchair. I was really skeptical about this because I'd been trying for months to pull myself into my chair from the ground, and I just couldn't do it. I had a profound fear of falling and being helpless, but no matter how much I practiced, I failed every time and resigned myself to the fact that the level of my injury made it impossible.

Still, I prayed, "God, give me strength to get into my chair." Before I knew what or how it happened, I was in my chair. I was overwhelmed with joy and the incredible intensity of God's presence. He heard my cry and gave me the strength I needed. I cried, and I laughed and enjoyed His love as it enveloped me.

I called Marv and told him I'd fallen, and before I could explain he said he'd be right home to get me. I had to interrupt him to tell him the rest of my story and all God had done for me. And then he cried.

Later that evening as we were revisiting my miracle, we wondered if the strength I'd received was just for that moment, or a permanent gift. (It's not unusual for supernatural strength to occur only in crisis situations.) Marv put me on the floor to try again, and to my delight, I lifted myself into my chair again and again. It was a miracle for keeps!

But all falls are not the same.

God often speaks to me while I'm on the floor and unable to move or run away. He knows that's where I'm perfectly still before Him, and He has my full attention. When I stop struggling and just snuggle up to Jesus and allow Him to love and comfort me in His tender arms, my relationship with Him grows the most dramatically.

I had another experience with falling after I'd come home from a routine shopping trip to Costco. It was about 3:30 in the afternoon when I pulled into our carport with a trunk full of groceries to put away. Once that was done, I planned on lying down for a short rest before preparing for the next day's Bible study. (Even though I'm paralyzed, my buns will burn if I sit for too long!)

Once again, God had another plan.

As I transferred from my car to my wheelchair, something went wrong, and I ended up on the carport floor. But the way I landed between the car door and my wheelchair kept me from pulling myself up. I didn't have a phone, and Marv wouldn't be home for two hours. I was alone. I needed to put away groceries. I needed to lie down. I needed to prepare for the Bible study. I needed help. I needed God.

I asked God to heal me and help me walk away from this insane situation. He didn't. I prayed He'd help me get in my chair. He wouldn't. I pleaded that He'd send someone to help me. I got the dog and the cat. Where was God? Was He even listening to me? I was hurt. I was helpless. I was alone, and I hated this predicament.

Eventually I stopped struggling and asked God to comfort and sustain me. I acknowledged His presence and begged Him to hold me. And He did. Jesus wrapped His tender arms around me and held me and comforted me as only He can do. There were no words or actions. It was just His mighty arms of love. I was safe, protected, and peaceful.

When Marv got home and discovered my desperate situation, he picked me up and carried me inside, and I cried. I cried tears of thankfulness for being tenderly held in Jesus' arms and tears of thankfulness for being tenderly held in Marv's arms. Nothing else mattered now, not the groceries, the Bible study, or my aching buns. I'd been held by my Master and Savior. I'd had another experience of falling but with a very different and very awesome ending.

It was finally sinking in that God allowed each of these circumstances so He could show me more of Himself, His power, His grace, His presence, and His love. My amazing journey was just beginning.

Unfortunately that wasn't the only time I failed to transfer successfully from my car to my wheelchair.

Jeanie and I always spent Wednesdays together. We'd shop, have lunch at a restaurant, and share our hearts. I always tried to be home by three o'clock so I could rest, read, and enjoy quiet time with Jesus, but one day my list of errands and shopping was particularly long, and I overexerted myself. It was after four o'clock when I got home, and I was exhausted. Then, as I attempted to transfer out of the car and into my chair, I fell. It was like déjà vu of my other fall. I sat on the carport floor alone, unable to pull myself up. The concrete was cold and hard. And just like before, I was humiliated, embarrassed, and frustrated. I was powerless to help myself or change my situation. Then Bronco meandered by, and I thought, *Oh my gosh! I'm eye to eye with the dog!*

Marv, my faithful knight in shining armor, was in Santa Barbara and unavailable, but since my last fall, he'd installed a phone in my car, so I called my daughter Jolene. While I waited for her, I prayed Psalm 23: *"The Lord is my shepherd; I shall not want ..."* I felt Him sustaining me. I continued praying, and when I got to, *"You prepare a table before me in the presence of my enemies ..."* I stopped and wondered who my enemies were.

Then it dawned on me that my thoughts were my enemies. I harbored self-loathing attitudes and thoughts in my heart. I resented my paralyzed body. I viewed it as a trap and a prison that failed miserably at everything I wanted it to do. I hated my circumstances and begrudged my never-ending dependency on others. I was in my forties, stranded pitifully on the garage floor, and there was nothing I could do about it. All those old familiar beliefs and feelings of failure, shame, and hopelessness that I'd grown up with flooded my mind. My thoughts were my fiercest enemies, and they were on the attack.

Then I considered the words *"You have prepared a table for me,"* and I wondered how that applied to me. Since "prepare" means to go before, then the Lord must have gone before me and prepared a place for me to sit at His table. And since God is all-knowing and ever-present, then preparation had been made for me, for this moment in time. God was intimately aware of my circumstances and all that was in my mind and heart.

Then I heard Him ask me to come and sit with Him.

"So often you pass by Me without a glance," He said. "I've prepared a table just for you. Please, Margaret, stay and sit with Me. I want to be with you and enjoy time with you. I've prepared a beautiful meal, and you are My guest of honor."

He knew I felt foolish and helpless, but He insisted that this was a divine appointment. I confessed my grief regarding my broken body, and my disgust of my broken life, and He reminded me that He created me and that He loved me. I admitted my humiliation, and He understood. I expressed my loneliness and seeming uselessness, and He invited me to experience the ultimate relationship with Him. And when I protested that my long-suffering was unbearable, He gently explained that it was necessary for me to endure so that I would learn to appreciate His profound love and compassion. He told me He was with me and for me, and He would be my steadfast Source for true rest.

Softly, I slipped into His rest. My spirit quieted, and I snuggled up in His tender care.

I was humbled by His grace and sought His forgiveness for believing Satan's destructive lies. Jesus was waiting for me and longed to commune with me as much as I longed to be with Him.

Jolene arrived about twenty minutes after my call, and in that short time frame, my frenzied anxiety had vanished and been replaced with complete peace.

I'd been in the presence of God. I'd sat with Him at His table and devoured His immeasurable love. Me—a lowly and lonely broken child of God—had been served by the King.

> *Ah, Lord GOD! It is you who has made the heavens and the earth by your great power and by your outstretched arm! Nothing is too hard for you.*
>
> —Jeremiah 32:17

In His Hands

Are your imperfections a source of embarrassment? Do you have scars that are a constant reminder of a past tragedy? Do you routinely take time to ponder all that Jesus' nail-scarred hands signify?

One of the most frustrating things for me remains the inability to accomplish all those things that I always took for granted. Things such as buttoning a blouse, zipping my trousers, unscrewing a jar, and opening a bottle are huge challenges for me. Picking up the toothpicks that Marv drops is nearly impossible, and I struggle with picking up a coin, putting on earrings, turning a page, shaking hands, and opening mail. (Just imagine trying to open mail with your hands in fists. I've learned to do it using my teeth, but it's still a major challenge!) Dropping and spilling things bring more helpless moments that I need to constantly work at to overcome. I feel so awkward and frustrated, and so very … disabled!

My acquired clumsiness can really test my patience. If I could choose, I'd choose functional hands rather than functional legs. And for the longest time I was doubly ashamed of my crippled hands because they looked terrible. I always did my best to hide them.

Then I read an article by Dr. Paul Brand, a world-renowned hand surgeon known for his innovative treatment for those suffering with leprosy, and it changed my attitude. Dr. Brand's expertise was not only in reconstructive surgery on the disfigured hands and feet of diabetics and victims of leprosy, but he also had an uncanny ability to look into the eyes of a person's soul and discern how to best meet their individual needs.

The article was a recap of one of Dr. Brand's presentations to those who'd suffered with leprosy. In it he elaborated on how the condition of peoples' hands (whether calloused or soft, meticulously manicured or ragged) revealed much about them and their lifestyle. He also noted that people with leprosy are prone to hide their disfigured hands.

I immediately understood.

Then he added that he would have loved to have seen Jesus' hands; His hands as an infant—so new and small and helpless; His hands as a boy—clumsily holding a brush, trying to form the letters of the alphabet; His hands as a carpenter—calloused, bruised, and splintered from working in carpentry; and His hands as the Great Physician and Healer—compassionate and sensitive hands whose touch radiated divine love; wonderfully tender hands that touched the blind, the diseased, and the needy. He would have liked to have seen Jesus' crucified hands—hands that experienced the excruciating pain of nails ruthlessly pounded through them; and finally, His resurrected hands—hands that still displayed the holes that Thomas insisted on feeling.

It's amazing that although Jesus' body was completely healed after His resurrection, the scars in His hands and feet and side remained.

The wounds of Jesus' humanity remained as evidence of His true identity and proof of His resurrection. They are an everlasting reminder of how He suffered once, for all. As He suffered for us, we are called to suffer for Him. He longs to identify with those who suffer and affirm that He knows, and He understands their torment. There's no pain or suffering we can endure that exceeds or even comes close to the pain and suffering that Jesus endured on the cross on our behalf. The proof is still visible in His hands.

Jesus could have risen from the grave with a flawless body, but He didn't. His scars remained traceable and remind us that He identifies with our pain. He understands our imperfections. He fought the same battles we fight that leave us physically, emotionally, and mentally scarred.

As Dr. Brand concluded his presentation, all the disfigured hands in his audience were lifted up and praised God. There'd be no more hiding and no more shame because of their deformities. Their hands were raised high in dignity, not to the famous hand surgeon, but to the Surgeon who restores poise, assurance, and peace.

Jesus identifies with us always. He is with us throughout all our frustrations, in the midst of all our shame and pain, and during all our losses. My life rests securely in His nail-scarred hands. No matter my circumstance or insecurity, He is with me, and He commiserates.

> *For I, the LORD your God, hold your right hand; it is I who say to you, "Fear not, I am the one who helps you."*
> —Isaiah 41:13

Walls

*What walls have you constructed in your mind, and
what do they hide? Why have you chosen to hide
these emotions rather than lay them on the altar
before God? Is there anger, fear, sadness,
or resentment that you've buried and
allowed to become sour?*

One night I dreamed that I was playing baseball and my team was winning by one run. Then someone unexpectedly put a barrier up around the infield. It was crazy! You can't play baseball with walls closing off the outfield!

The next morning as I remembered my dream, the thought of walls intrigued me. Some walls provide safety and protection, while others are perfect for hiding behind. And some walls are just huge obstacles, impossible to navigate around. I've often used walls as a crutch to make me feel protected, but in actuality I think they've been a deterrent in my healing process.

Through the years, God has used very specific times and events to mend and renew my mind. One in particular happened on a summer evening in 1994. I vividly remember the time and the place when one of the walls I'd been carelessly leaning on crumbled and left me dazed and amazed.

Marv, Jeanie, her husband, George, and I were going to visit the *Atocha* shipwreck presentation and then go out for dinner. The *Atocha* was a Spanish ship that sank off the coast of Florida in 1622 while attempting to navigate hurricane-force winds and rain. The ship, all its crew, passengers, and precious cargo—enormous amounts of gold, silver, and jewels—were lost. Explorers discovered the massive sunken treasure in 1990 and traveled the country to share its history and display some of the booty they'd retrieved.

Dad's jewelry store was selected as the site to display the ship's precious cargo, and the antique shop next door was selected to show the film. (The antique shop had replaced the gift shop I'd managed for so many years.)

When we arrived at Dad's store, the familiarity of the mahogany showcases elegantly presenting the glistening gems, and the smell and feel of the rich thick carpet was profound and stirred up wonderful memories; memories of selling beautiful china, crystal, and sterling silver flatware; memories of decorating windows, buying trips, and meeting interesting people; and memories of self-confidence, accomplishments, and tackling exciting challenges. Most of my family members had worked at the store at one time or another. For me, there was an undeniable sense of value and security associated with this store. As I looked around I visualized how our patrons had meandered between the gift shop and the jewelry store by way of two large openings. The two stores were connected and yet separate.

As I reminisced I longed for everything to be as it was. I wanted to be like those solid, beautiful, rich showcases. But I'd changed. My body had changed. And the changes were permanent. My broken neck had locked up my body and bound me to a wheelchair.

Trying to push my wheelchair through the plush carpet was difficult. As people filled the store, my vantage point grew more cluttered and viewing the treasures was nearly impossible. I felt lost in what had once been my home away from home.

Nevertheless I was excited to go next door and see the film in my old gift-shop stomping grounds. But humiliation enveloped me almost instantly as I tried to wheel around the crowd already seated. I needed help pushing across the carpet. People had to move their chairs for me to squeeze by, and everyone stared at me. My clumsiness and awkwardness seemed magnified as I bumped into everything in my path. The room was so packed that the four of us couldn't sit together. I'd never felt so alone in the midst of such a crowd.

Once I was settled, I looked around at the place where I'd spent so much of my life. I searched for things that time hadn't altered. I gazed at the roof, the balcony, the carpet, and the walls. And then it hit me that the walls had changed. A permanent wall had been erected where there'd once been openings connecting the two stores. Immediately, my thoughts turned to another aspect of my life, one that had once been openly connected with but was now barricaded by a permanent wall.

I'll never forget the finality and the devastation I felt when the doctor said, "You'll never walk again. You'll sit in a wheelchair for the rest of your life. You're permanently disabled."

The walls in my mind screamed at me. They blocked so much of what I longed for. They fenced me off from the life I'd loved. The me that I'd loved. And the worst part was that I'd designed and built them myself. I'd blocked out so many of my emotions and sadness. I'd determined to be strong for others, hide my tears, and live up to the expectations of the poster someone gave me while in rehab that admonished me to make lemonade out of the bushel of lemons sitting on my frozen lap.

The walls around the baseball field in my dream didn't belong there, and neither did the walls I'd built around my mind. It was time to mourn my losses and let the walls fall where they would. It was time to heal, time to unlock the door and free all the emotions I'd been hiding. My mind raced while the movie played. I knew an immense wall was about to implode within me. All those things I'd hidden for so long were bubbling up and destroying the barrier I'd erected.

My former independence of moving, walking, running, bending, standing, reaching, and grasping without a second thought now required enormous amounts of forethought, planning, and effort. Now I needed equipment, people, batteries, wheels, special reaching devices, and an adapted car with hand controls. The reminders of all these losses still recur daily. Hourly. Every minute has to be thought through. Every potential circumstance of helplessness and frustration has to be anticipated and thwarted.

Growing up, I was conditioned to take an aspirin when life got tough. Rocking the boat in our family just wasn't acceptable. Even as an adult, I assumed that if I allowed myself to cry, grieve or be angry, then it would be a permanent condition—like a tattoo. I'd concluded that since my physical disability was permanent, then any emotional "malfunctions" would be permanent.

Even before the movie ended and our evening out was over, I sensed the wall between my mind and my body start to crumble. But once I got home that wall of grief came down in an avalanche of pebbles and debris, and it piled at my feet. God held the chisel that freed what had been contained.

> *But now, O LORD, you are our Father; we are the clay,*
> *and you are our potter; we are all the work of your hand.*
> —Isaiah 64:8

Almighty God assured me that He knew all that had been suffered and lost, not only for me, but for my family as well. In an instant, my girls lost the mom they'd always known, and my heart ached for them. My parents experienced overwhelming grief and helplessness in trying to put me back together again. Their love was constant, but they carried a tremendous burden of responsibility toward me. Although Marv had discovered a place, a calling, and a willingness to love me unconditionally, he'd lost the cute, able-bodied, independent gal that I'd been. He'd become my hands and my feet.

I mourned the loss of my gift shop, the job I'd loved so much. And for the first time I allowed myself the freedom to feel angry at the drunk driver who forced me off the road, but who claimed (according to the police report) that I had been in his way. As a result of his poor choice of drinking too much and driving out of control, my life was forever out of my control. Now the injustices of life were larger than life itself. I'd obeyed the rules; he hadn't. I had a lifetime of pain and anguish ahead of me, and he was freed from prison after six months for his good behavior. But my good behavior wouldn't free me from my prison.

I cried in Jesus' arms that night and allowed the sunken grief of my losses to surface. As God excavated these tender realities in my life, I reflected on the precious treasures amid the ruins of the *Atocha*. It was amazing how God orchestrated the two events in my life. Those valuable treasures that brought me freedom and relief and wholeness bubbled up from the depths of my soul. In the process, I was able to surrender my life and my desire to control myself to God and to His will for my life. I'd found God hidden in the deep and came to know and experience Him there—deeper still.

> *How great are your works, O LORD! Your thoughts are very deep.*
>
> —Psalm 92:5

It was okay to be sad and angry. God understood, acknowledged, and identified with my grief. It was good to pour out my sorrows on Jesus. He'd known them all along. It was necessary to vent my anger on Jesus, so He could help me move on.

My walls were man-made, by me or others in my life, just as the walls in the antique store were man-made. As God dredged up my feelings and brought them to the surface, and as He crumbled the walls that hid me and numbed my pain, He spiritually reminded me that He had collapsed every wall and nothing separates me from His love, acceptance, great empathy, and comfort. God's ever-gentle, gracious, healing hand found my sunken treasure. I'm still disabled, still confined in my wheelchair, and still experiencing losses daily, but now I'm storing up my treasures in heaven. Now I'm more open and honest and free to express my feelings without fear. Now, I let God hide me and guard me in the bottomless priceless treasure of His peace.

> *But lay up for yourselves treasures in heaven, where neither moth nor rust destroys and where thieves do not break in and steal.*
>
> —Matthew 6:20

The Perfect Worship

*Whom and what do you turn to for solace in place of
Jesus? Do they provide you with perfectly satisfying
and long-lasting comfort, peace and joy, or
are they just temporary quick-fixes?*

Since I've come to know Jesus, I've always looked forward to Sundays and the promise of a wonderful time of worship and praise under the leadership of our pastor. They are special times in my week when I feel safe and relaxed in God's presence. But one week as I left the sanctuary I had a longing for something more. Nevertheless, I headed down the hall to teach the first- through third-grade children. Teaching these eager young hearts was one of my favorite things to do, and I was prepared and excited to share Jesus' love with them. And yet on this particular morning I felt an unusual uneasiness.

I didn't realize it at the time, but in the next moment the reason for my uneasiness was standing in front of me asking if he could help me with my class. At the last minute, I said "yes," and that's when all my lesson plans went out the window. This sixteen-year-old young man dominated my class and the result was absolute chaos.

By the time Sunday school was over, I was more than anxious to escape. I was desperate to seek and spend time with my precious Savior. It didn't matter where—I just needed Jesus.

Once I got home, I thought an evening movie (with popcorn, of course) would settle me down. But the movie was lousy, and the popcorn was burnt. So I attempted my tried-and-true solution for drowning my disappointments—a nice hot bath. As I floated in the water and read some psalms, I felt my anxiety lift and be replaced with the serenity of God's holy presence.

Then I turned over to my stomach, one of the few things I can typically manage on my own. Except this particular night something went terribly wrong. I lost my balance, and my peace was instantly transformed into full-fledged panic. Marv came to my rescue, but it was just one more thing that day that went wrong. I couldn't wait to get into bed, hide under the covers, and pray away this disastrous day. It seemed that the more I longed for fulfillment, the more I received torment.

Finally, I was nearly settled in bed and my dear Marv was helping me lie down and adjusting my bed-bag. Peace was just a breath away.

Or so I thought. As Marv made the last adjustment with my bed-bag, the tube came loose and urine started flying everywhere. It was much too late to change the sheets. I was lying in my own urine and far from the refuge and comfort I'd sought in my bed.

Then God reminded me that He is my sole refuge. All day I'd been foolishly trying to find Him and His unsurpassable peace in all those other things and places. And finally, about midnight, I heard Him whisper that nothing and no one can take His place.

In perfect worship, I finally got it. God is my all-sufficient refuge.

> In you, O LORD, do I take refuge; let me never be put to shame; in your righteousness deliver me!
> —Psalm 31:1

On this beautiful Sunday morning, I had carried all my hopes for perfect worship in broken and leaky cisterns, and they had dried up along the way. Only the Spirit of Christ Himself could satisfy the longing in my soul. Christ and Christ alone is worthy of my worship.

Letting Go

What special person(s) in your life have you had to let go? Were you able to spend precious and tender time together in their last moments? Are there people in your life who seem to block your path to Jesus?

Throughout the years some of my most treasured times were spent visiting Nana. Although my visits with her when I was a little girl became less frequent after we moved across town, it didn't diminish our love for each other. She had always been and continued to be my confidante. I could chat with her about anything, including my mistakes, my poor choices, and my disability, and she listened without a harsh word or critical heart. Her love was unconditional and beyond any I'd ever known.

In her later years she moved to Oceano, a small town about twenty miles away from my home. I made every effort to take my girls to visit her weekly so they, too, could experience her gentle love. She lived in a storybook red cottage with a white picket fence across the front yard. It was precious—just as she was precious.

As Nana aged and her body began to fail, my heart began to break. I couldn't stand the thought of losing her. Her love was such a huge part of my life. When her days were literally numbered, I had the opportunity to pray with her, assuring her that she was heaven-bound and on her way to see Jesus. Then we made a date to go on a long walk on heaven's streets of gold. But none of the promises of heaven comforted my broken heart or eased the pain of letting her go.

One night I dreamed of her. She was in bed and asked me to get her a drink of water to quench her thirst. I walked (only in my dream) to her kitchen, and when I returned to her room it was full of people, doctors, nurses, and photographers. I couldn't get the glass of water to her. I pushed and shoved, and panic overtook me. Suddenly, Nana came to me. She was whole and healthy. Then she placed her loving, soft pink hands on my cheeks and said, "I love you, Margaret Ann. God bless you. The Lord's hand is on you and your girls, and on Melby Lynn and Donald."

While I was still dreaming I was awakened by the phone. It was Dad. Nana had just died. I was stunned. God sent Nana to me on her way to heaven to give me exactly what I needed to let her go—one last gift of her amazing love and the assurance of heaven. I clung to that gift in the days to come as my heart swelled with the pain of losing her. As I recall her now, I still feel her warm, loving hands on my face comforting me and assuring me of her everlasting love.

So now faith, hope, and love abide, these three; but the greatest of these is love.
—1 Corinthians 13:13

The Gift

*Even though you may have already accepted Jesus' gift of
salvation, have you accepted His gift of Himself? Do you
seek Jesus for what He gives, or do you seek Him
for who He is? Have you ever considered that
what you may view as a personal limitation,
God may view as a perfect instrument to
reveal Himself to others?*

It was 2001. Twenty-six years since my accident. Twenty-six years of living wheelchair bound. I'd experienced times of joy in God's presence and contentedly nestled in His peace and protection. I'd also experienced times of earnest seeking and growing in my relationship with Him. And there were also times when I'd run away from Him and done my best to forget He even existed.

But there was one particular time that was fraught with frustration and anger unlike any I'd felt before. I was fed up with my crummy existence. I cried out to God that I was tired of living in a wheelchair. I'd spent nearly half my life coping and struggling with my paralysis, and that was enough. I wanted something more in my life. I needed something more. I'd recently seen a film that depicted Jesus healing the lepers, the lame, and the blind. Why wouldn't He heal me, too? I needed an answer.

So I waited.

And when God finally spoke, He told me that my disability was a gift.

A gift? Was He kidding? I was so angry! I'd managed a gift shop for several years, and by all outward appearances my paralysis wasn't a gift. A gift is something beautiful, carefully covered in attractive wrapping paper with a bow regally crowning the top. It's something that brings joy and excitement to the recipient.

And God said, "Open My gift."

I didn't think His gift was beautifully wrapped. I thought it was thrown together with scraps of rubber tires, screws, spokes, malfunctioning hands, and limp, useless legs. I mentally tore off this ugly packaging and scanned the inside, but all I found was more ugliness—the ugliness of long-suffering, loss, and loneliness, and the ugliness of pain, failure, grief, anger, self-imposed rejection, and self-pity.

And then I looked deeper and tucked in the heart of this crumpled mess I found my gift. It was Jesus. My custom-made gift from God was Jesus. My ongoing helplessness and hardship kept me dependent on Jesus and not on myself. Jesus is my most precious gift. He is my gift of hope, sustenance, and strength. He is my source of peace, joy, grace, mercy, and love. Jesus is my never-ending daily manna who gives me life and breath. He supplies me with wisdom and holds my future in His capable, mighty hands. I don't have to depend on my crippled hands, and I don't have to depend on my paralyzed legs. Jesus is my true support, my all in all, now and forever. Jesus is the perfect and beautiful gift who lives within my heart.

My gift did bring me excitement and joy. In fact, I was flooded with joy. I grew deeper in the knowledge of Christ in me. I had a new appreciation and thankfulness for God's mysterious ways. God opened my eyes and heart to see the beauty of Christ and accept the gift of His immeasurable grace to live another day with Jesus.

My gift was Jesus, beautifully wrapped in everlasting life and crowned King of kings and Lord of lords.

After I finished opening my gift, Jesus showed me something else that I'd never before imagined would be possible.

Maybe I was a gift, too.

I'd grown up thinking that outward beauty and flawlessness was what was most important. When I worked in the gift shop, I wrapped packages in shiny paper and big beautiful bows to make them more enticing. But when Jesus gave me the gift of Himself, I realized that gifts are tempting and enticing no matter what they're wrapped in.

Suddenly it occurred to me that others might actually be drawn to Jesus because I'm not clothed in perfection. Maybe people could be drawn to Him because I'm clothed with external limitations, imperfections, and disabilities. I finally understood that these wrappings—these rubber wheels and spokes and crooked hands—could be the very tools God uses in my life to demonstrate the power of Christ in me. I discovered that all the stares and attention drawn to me because of my weaknesses might be divinely orchestrated opportunities to share what and who is inside me.

> *Every good gift and every perfect gift is from above, coming down from the Father of lights with whom there is no variation or shadow due to change.*
> —James 1:17

What a marvelous revelation!

Enlarge My Faith

*What comes to mind during those times when you're feel-
ing pitiful and singled out? Have you ever wondered
if your faith is adequate and your repentance is
acceptable? Do you hunger and thirst for more
faith? Who do you look to for your supply,
and who are your role models?*

As my faith in God continues to deepen and grow, it continually
undergoes an assortment of challenges, tests, and refinement.
The questions of "why me?" and "why not me?" still come to mind
even though my accident happened many years ago.

I watch as God's Holy Spirit heals so many lost souls. I hear people
pray and see the evidence of God's power as He mends broken, ailing,
and hurting bodies. I witness how He miraculously brings others closer
to Him, and how He's glorified in the process. I feel the authority of
Almighty God as He tangibly grabs hold of the next generation and
commissions them to carry forth His Gospel. I continue to see and
hear the miraculous testimonies of new believers. I savor the excitement and expectancy as God's hand moves in lives, in communities,
and in the world.

And yet there are many like me who haven't been physically healed,
and I wonder what God's message is to us. To me. I wonder what He
holds in His heart for those of us who haven't received the answers
we've hoped for in our prayers, prayers we've desperately, tearfully,
and repeatedly offered.

And I sometimes question whether my faith is adequate, or if my repentance is acceptable. I wonder if my prayers are misguided. I just don't understand why God allowed me to be a member of this small disabled community and chose not to reinstate my natural physical health.

I know my Father knows best, and I shouldn't ask Him "why?" but I do. "Why me?" still occasionally creeps into my mind and heart, and so far, God hasn't answered. Then again, sometimes I'm afraid that if He did answer, it would be something I might not want to hear. Maybe my question to God should be "what" is happening as I still sit—still broken, still waiting, still desperate, and still ever so needy.

During these times I plead for God's help to keep me from falling, not out of my chair, but out of my place in His presence and into the sins of condemnation, unbelief, or flimsy faith.

I diligently follow God's lead and pursue His Word. The times I spend in fellowship with other saints serving, worshipping, and glorifying Jesus are priceless. I'd be foolish to discount the tremendous restoration God has generously bestowed on me through the years. He's held me together daily in life's most minute details. My sovereign Lord has met my practical needs by maintaining the nuts and bolts and mechanisms of my wheelchair. God alone is the reason infections haven't constantly ravaged my body. God alone is responsible for annihilating so many feelings of rejection, fear, and jealousy. And God alone gets the credit for demolishing my codependent, critical spirit.

And yet I hunger for more.

God's powerful Holy Spirit continually lavishes me with His grace to face each new day. His supernatural strength tirelessly carries me. The life of Christ gently flows through my veins and sustains me. There isn't a part of me or of my life that is devoid of the presence of Christ. Just as the ocean's waves keep coming ashore, so God's faithfulness comes to me.

And still, I thirst for more.

When I'm feeling disheartened and dejected, people often encourage me to "keep asking, keep moving forward, keep believing, and keep developing my faith." I'm often amazed at how others long to witness the life-sized obvious miracles that God performs and rarely appreciate the more personal unseen and unheard everyday miracles that are just as profound. I'm always saddened when people refuse to acknowledge the unnoticed world and the immense faith required to wait patiently on the Lord when He seems elusive. Blind faith that trusts God when He seems absent and silent is true faith. It's that kind of faith that's impossible to muster up on my own that I rely on for healing. It's that faith, that perfect vital gift from God, that I can't live without.

Even though God hasn't physically healed me, He unwaveringly provides me with the faith I need to accept His answers to my pleas, regardless of what those answers may be. He permeates me with faith that carries me through shattered dreams and onward to the next day. He injects me with unshakable faith that doesn't yield to sickness, as yet unanswered prayer and imperceptible healing. God saturates me with limitless faith to represent Him as He continually renews me through and in spite of my burden.

> Now faith is the assurance of things hoped for, the convic-
> tion of things not seen.
> —Hebrews 11:1

Hebrews 11:1 isn't a definition. It's a description of how faith works.

Patriots such as Moses, Abraham, and Noah are wonderful role models of great faith. They didn't abandon God even though His directives and promises seemed far-fetched. God promised to part the Red Sea for Moses and his followers. God promised Abraham that he'd become the father of many nations when he was 100 years old. God told Noah to build an ark in preparation for the flood before he'd ever seen rain. All these men and many others followed God's direction when it seemed foolish and against the odds. And yet their faith remained strong until their dying days. Each one died still embracing and ever assured of the promises of heaven. Each one died acknowledging that he was but a pilgrim on earth, just passing through to his heavenly home.

There are countless biblical saints who followed in the faith-full footsteps of the patriots listed in Hebrews 11, and many of them were tortured, mocked, scourged, stoned, and slain by the sword. They died without seeing their promises fulfilled, and yet their faith never wavered. They possessed model faith.

The faith of our fathers didn't produce a remedy or a miraculous healing; rather, it sustained them. It carried them through their anguish and seeming hopelessness. The same faith that enables some to escape trouble enables others to endure it. The same faith that delivers some from suffering and death enables others to die victoriously.

And the same faith that's present when someone else is mended is the same faith that enables me to live in brokenness and affliction. Faith works in both extremes and in everything in between. Faith, in and of itself, is so much deeper and wider than my mind can conceive or my words can express. But it resonates with my spirit, and all is well with my soul if God chooses not to heal me because I know He supplies my faith as I carry on.

Be glorified, precious Jesus, in my brokenness or in my healing. Faith is alive in both.

The apostles said to the Lord, "Increase our faith!"
—Luke 17:5

Hands and Feet

*Are you available for God, no matter what? Does being
accessible to God so He can further His Kingdom top
your list of priorities every single day? Does your
dance with Him flow without distractions?*

One of Marv's favorite hobbies is target-shooting with pistols, rifles, and shotguns that were used in the Old West. He's competed in many tournaments throughout our marriage and always enjoys them. Fortunately the contests are typically close by so he doesn't have to do a lot of traveling or be away from home for too long. But one year there was a special tournament in New Mexico he just couldn't resist enrolling in.

At the time, we'd been married for twenty-seven years and had never been apart for more than two or three days, so this was a big decision. He and two friends ultimately decided to make the fourteen-hour drive together and determined they'd be gone for six days. I wanted him to go and participate in his sport but I also knew that it would come at a high price for me.

Besides loving Marv and loving our life together, he is my hands and feet in countless ways. Our life has evolved into a dance. We know our steps and we waltz gracefully through our days without too many stumbles. I rarely have to ask Marv to do anything for me. His tender care comes automatically.

It was hard for Marv to leave me and entrust others with my care (Marv's boundless love still leaves me speechless), and it had become more difficult for me to receive assistance from others. So the battle in my mind raged. I was angry that I was so needy and dependent, but I realized that this was God's plan, and He had a purpose for carrying it out. So I surrendered. I waved the white flag and conceded, "Your will, Lord, not mine."

While Marv was gone, Jolene, and her husband, Steve, spent time with me. Jeanie came over one night, and Maureen stayed another night. We all had special moments together, but I became weary of having to verbalize all my needs. Where Marv routinely "pushed, pulled, and zipped," others needed direction and instruction.

One morning as I waited for Jolene to come get me out of bed, I had the terrifying thought that if she didn't show up, my life for that day would be fruitless and useless. I needed her to get me out of bed and get me going. I needed her hands and feet. Then I thought of my heavenly Father looking down on me and thinking the same thing.

If Margaret doesn't show up today to be My hands and feet, not much is going to happen through her for My Kingdom.

And I truly saw how God needs me to show up. He needs me to be prayerfully available so He can use me to be His hands and His feet in this broken world. It's His strength and assistance, His wisdom and counsel, that I rely on to carry out the tasks He sets before me. Such a spirit of humility washed over me as I pondered the necessity of being dependent on God so that His power may be magnified.

As I wait for others to tend to me, I'm enveloped and filled with a spirit of love. As I wait on the Lord, He becomes everything I need in order to accomplish His perfect will. As I wait on Jesus, I have the privilege of experiencing God's beautiful, supernatural Spirit-filled living.

I'm so thankful to Jesus for teaching me another valuable lesson. It's simple yet profound and revitalizing. I'm so thankful to my heavenly Father for supplying so many willing hands that unselfishly reach out to me in times of need. And I'm so thankful to Christ that He forgives me of my prideful, self-sufficient spirit. The ways of my precious Lord are so much deeper than I can possibly comprehend.

As for me, I would seek God, and to God would I commit my cause, who does great things and unsearchable, marvelous things without number.

—Job 5:8–9

I was so excited when Marv finally came home. For days I'd been eagerly anticipating the moment when I could fall into his arms and rest. When he got home he said that he'd had a great trip. At the age of seventy-one, he'd still managed to shoot seventh overall in his class worldwide. He also finished first in high-speed pistol shooting worldwide. (He still hits the mark!) But the best part of his return was resuming our dance and waltzing through the steps that God divinely choreographs. The music, composed and orchestrated by God, is our song. And it is too beautiful for lyrics.

Divine Messengers

Whom has God used as a divine messenger in your life?
Do you think you have ever been one?

I'm continually amazed at the creative ways God brings salvation into lives. And I'm especially amazed when He utilizes divine messengers to accomplish His will. My dad's story fits that category. He would have loved to have shared it himself, but he's already in heaven with Jesus, so I'll share it on his behalf.

After I became a Christian in 1979, I knew Dad needed Jesus. He didn't need religion, or works, or success; he just needed Jesus. Dad acknowledged God, but only from a distance. Dad controlled his life and made his own decisions, both personal and professional. He was a good man, he was full of integrity and wisdom, and he had an uncanny ability for financial prosperity. Dad was devoted to his family, friends, and fellow Rotarians. He was multifaceted and enjoyed golf, hunting, farming, socializing, investing, and gambling. He embraced people and loved genuinely. And whenever Dad gave, he gave generously.

In the early 1960s, Dad was drawn to Mormonism. (Many of Mom's family members were raised in the Mormon religion.) With Dad's lead, we all learned the teachings of the Mormon faith and were baptized. (Dad was immersed twice because his big toe wasn't completely submerged the first time!) We had family devotions, participated in seminary, and attended church. But when it came to abstaining from drinking alcohol and smoking cigarettes, Dad drew the line. That was asking too much for Mom and him. So while Maureen, Mark, and I reluctantly continued with our religious obligations, our spiritual journey as a family ended.

Eventually Dad became a "Jack Mormon"—someone who claims to be a Mormon but has run away from practicing all the protocol. The only thing Dad remained faithful to was tithing. Through the years, Dad remained stoic in spite of the countless tragedies, deaths, drinking, and ups and downs that life presented.

Once I converted to Christianity, I began praying and interceding for my family. And in December 1999, the holy God of the universe touched Dad's heart in a truly extraordinary way.

Mom's death was imminent, and all of our immediate family members gathered to be with her and with Dad. We'd congregated at 419, the house across from the Miller Street School that we'd grown up in. Mark was the only one who wasn't with us because he'd had to step out for an important annual consultation with Hugh, a business associate from Nebraska.

As we all sat there, I quietly embraced all that Mom was to me. I treasured all the beautiful and selfless qualities she possessed. She was always so spontaneously fun-loving. We never knew when she might initiate a wild Ping-Pong game of "drop the paddle" or a water or mud fight. She loved gardening; and she was a terrific cook and an expert housekeeper. She loved to sing, she was quick to recite a dramatic art tale she'd learned as a child, and she always looked like a million dollars.

But even more than that, she loved people. She made certain everyone felt welcome in her home, and she never hesitated to take a home-cooked meal to someone who might be grieving, sick, or needy in some other way. She was a tremendous giver of her time and resources and stunningly beautiful both inside and out.

When Mom took her last breath, Dad leaned over and kissed her good-bye. He'd just lost the love of his life. We called Mark imme-diately, even though he was in a business meeting with Hugh. As it happened, Hugh was standing nearby and overheard the conversation. Then he asked if he could visit Dad, and Mark consented.

We were sitting in the living room awaiting the hearse to take Mom's body to the mortuary when the doorbell rang. I instantly thought the timing couldn't have been worse for a salesman or a visitor. It would have been such an intrusion on these solemn moments. But when Dad opened the door, it was Hugh.

Hugh was a born-again Christian and, in this case, a divine messenger. He'd felt God direct him to come and share the Gospel message with Dad. They stood on the doorstep and chatted for several minutes. And it was there, on the steps of 419, that Dad accepted the Lord into his heart.

When he came back inside he said, "I can't believe it's so simple to go to heaven. There'll be no more Mormonism is this family or at Mom's funeral."

I saw the walls tumble down. It was such a holy moment.

The next few days were understandably tough. We muddled through funeral arrangements and family decisions as our hearts ached with loss and grief. In the midst of it all, Dad received an unexpected call from my sixth-grade teacher and lifelong friend, Roberta. Roberta, a born-again Christian who currently lived in Texas, wanted to come for a visit after the funeral and other formalities were over. She wanted to come and comfort Dad, but she had one stipulation: he had to take her to the church I attended.

Dad was shocked and claimed the roof would surely cave in as soon as he set foot in the church. But Roberta persisted and promised to hold his hand.

When she came, Dad joined her at church, just as he'd promised. Roberta held Dad's hand as they entered, just as she'd promised. (He was amazed that the roof stayed intact!) And on this day, in this church, Dad experienced the unconditional love of Jesus. It was the first day of his spiritual journey, and it started with God's second divine messenger sitting by his side.

Dad grew tremendously in his faith during the next seven years. He rarely missed a Sunday of worship. He broke all his religious obligations with the Mormon church and allowed God to control his life.

We worshipped together, partook of the Lord's Supper together, and laughed and cried and journeyed together in our walk with God. It was such a precious and special blessing to share spiritually with Dad.

On October 8, 2006, when Dad's death was near, he was ready to meet the very One who'd created him. Steve and Jolene prayed for him and read Psalm 27.

> The LORD is my light and my salvation; whom shall I fear? The LORD is the stronghold of my life; of whom shall I be afraid?
>
> —Psalm 27:1

Dad was peaceful as he lay in the family room of 419. Worship songs softly played as we talked about those he'd soon see in heaven, and how he'd find his name written in the Book of Life. I touched his hands one last time and thanked him for being such a wonderful father to me.

That night as I was soaking in the tub and listening to my favorite radio station, the song "I Can Only Imagine," played. The lyrics ponder how we'll react when we see Jesus. Will we fall down and worship Him, or dance, or be still? I tried to picture what it was going to be like for Dad. And then the phone rang, and Mark announced that Dad had just died. The Lord had given me a brief peek of Dad being ushered into heaven.

Dad followed Jesus until he went home to live with Him forever. God orchestrated a beautiful divine plan to rescue Dad. He sent a faith-filled man from Nebraska and a faith-filled woman from Texas. God is so amazing.

Oh, how I thank God for saving Dad and for giving me a brief glimpse into the supernatural. And I especially thank God for divine messengers.

Pearl of Great Price

Are you the merchant in search of Jesus? Are you allowing Him to form you into a pearl of great price, and is He your pearl of great price?

For years I didn't like my name—Margaret. It means pearl, a jewel of great worth, but I always thought it sounded so formal and old-fashioned. And when I was younger, I certainly didn't consider myself formal or old-fashioned. Through the years, though, I've learned to understand my name and, of course, love pearls!

The process involved in the natural formation of a pearl is fascinating. When a tiny stone or a bit of sand gets inside the shell of an oyster or some other small mollusk, it becomes an irritant because it's a hard, foreign object in a naturally soft environment. In an effort to protect itself, the oyster secretes a lustrous substance called nacre that surrounds the object. A pearl is the product of layer upon layer of nacre coating the irritant.

When I considered my name, and looked at my life, I thought I must be the irritant to my parents. I was convinced that I'd been the ultimate mistake in their eyes. I wasn't like Maureen. I wasn't a good student. I got pregnant out of wedlock. I was divorced. And I was paralyzed. My name seemed to fit me like a glove.

I was a pearl formed by rubbing people the wrong way.

But after I was born again and became a new creation in Christ, and after I became a member of God's Kingdom, then I understood the truth of God, and I gained new and different insight regarding my name.

> *Again, the kingdom of heaven is like a merchant in search of fine pearls, who, on finding one pearl of great value, went and sold all that he had and bought it.*
> —Matthew 13:45–46

The merchant was me, and I was on a journey to find life. I was seeking the Author and Giver of life—everlasting life—Jesus Christ. Instantly, when Jesus entered my heart, my life, and my body, the Spirit of the living God was like a small grain of sand or a tiny mustard seed. Then, as life continually brought challenges, pressures, losses, celebrations, tears, joys, and hardships, layer upon layer of His truth formed around that small seed of faith. God slowly defined who I was in Christ, and I gradually sold all of Satan's lies. I exchanged every lie for the Word of God, and His truth began layering and forming a pearl of great price. The truth of God was setting me free.

> *Out of my distress I called on the LORD; the LORD answered me and set me free.*
> —Psalm 118:5

Finally, I knew I wasn't a mistake. I was part of His plan from the beginning of time. I wasn't designed to be like my sister, but to be exactly who God created me to be. God has forgiven and continues to forgive my mistakes, and He has redeemed those lost years and has used them to further His Kingdom. My accident was tragic, but not so tragic that He couldn't bring forth good from it.

Through year after year of adversity, a pearl of great price was formed in me, layer upon layer. That pearl of great price is Jesus, the Author and Finisher of my faith.

Back Row (left to right): Julie Page, John Page, Johnny Page, Kaitlyn Henry, Steve Henry, Jolene Henry, Stephen Henry, Curtis Henry
Middle Row (left to right): Leslie Henry, Jake Page, me, Marv, Josh Page
Front Row (left to right): Joelle Page, Jennifer Page

To order additional copies

a Pearl formed by adversity

have your credit card ready and call
1 800-917-BOOK (2665)

or e-mail
orders@selahbooks.com

or order online at
www.selahbooks.com

–